February 25, 1998

To: Alan

Love,

From: Dad & Your Mother

XXOO

You'll enjoy reading this book. Hitler was quite an intelligent man, but paranoid.

A PICTORIAL HISTORY OF
ADOLF HITLER

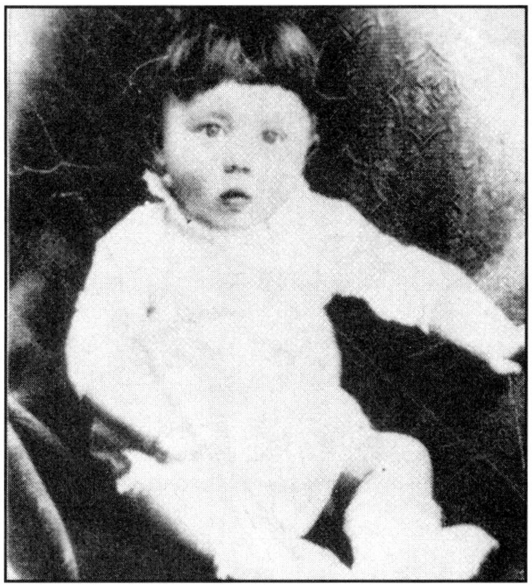

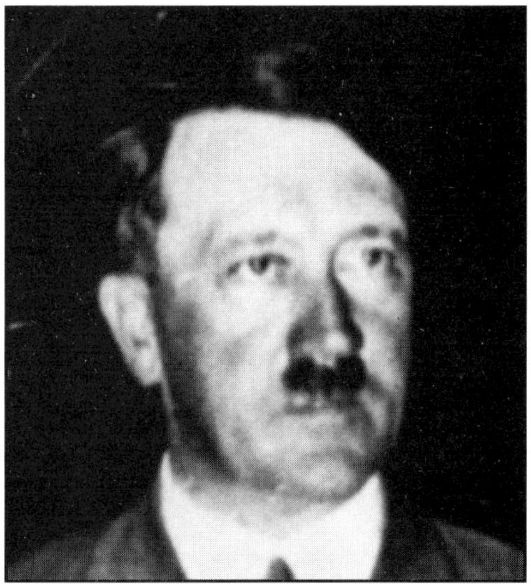

NIGEL BLUNDELL

JG PRESS

ACKNOWLEDGEMENTS

Photography with kind permission of The Science Museum/Science & Society Picture Library.
The publishers are also greatly indebted to Robert Mullett for his research work.

This edition produced 1995 by The Promotional Reprint Company Ltd
Deacon House, 65 Old Church Street
Chelsea, London SW3 5BS

Published in the USA 1995 by JG Press
Distributed by World Publications, Inc.

The JG Press imprint is a trademark of
JG Press, Inc.
455 Somerset Avenue
North Dighton, MA 02764

ISBN 1 57215 137 4

Printed and bound in Hong Kong

CONTENTS

Introduction

WHAT is the special ingredient that sets a man apart, that makes him a hero or a tyrant? Nero, Attila the Hun, Tamburlaine, Genghis Khan – they became legends of barbarity, albeit in a smaller world than today's.

They will forever remain enigmas, lost as they are in the mists of history. But what do we really know about a tyrant with more blood on his hands than any of these? A man who stands alone in the annals of tyranny? A man from our own, supposedly civilised century?

No one alive today is untouched by the deeds or the legacy of Adolf Hitler. He was responsible for the deaths of millions, not only on the battlefields of World War II, but also in the concentration camps, as he set about the conquest of Europe and the systematic genocide of the Jews.

Who was this seemingly undistinguished son of a minor customs official in provincial Austria, who rebuilt a German empire from the ashes of World War I defeat, then led his adoptive country into a new dark age?

Why did millions espouse the myth of an Aryan race of young, blond demigods when it was propounded by a squat, dark-haired man in poor health?

In 1938 after the seizure of Austria and the Sudetenland, Adolf Hitler was proclaimed "Man Of The Year" by Time magazine. Yet after six years of war his memory was reviled around the world.

Left: Hitler's mother, Klara, whom he revered.

Right: Hitler's father, Alois Shiklgruber, often cited as a cause of Hitler's ego-mania.

EARLY YEARS

CONTRARY to the story that gained credence during the war, Adolf Hitler was not illegitimate. His father, Alois Shiklgruber, was born out of wedlock. Alois had his own birth legitimised by persuading the local priest to alter his birth documents to give him his father's name of Hitler. (The confusion over Alois Hitler's documents allowed later detractors to allege that Adolf Hitler's real maternal grandfather had in fact been a Jew named Frankenberger, who had been in the household where Alois's mother, Maria Anna Shiklgruber, was in service.)

Adolf Hitler was born at 6.30pm on 20 April 1889 at Braunau-am-Inn in Austria. His mother, Klara, was Alois Hitler's third wife. Three other children of the union died in infancy; only a sister, Paula, survived. From his father's second marriage, there was a half-brother Alois and a half-sister Angela, later to become the housekeeper at Adolf's Bavarian retreat of Berchtesgaden.

Hitler was born in this building in Braunau-am-Inn, Austria, on 20 April 1889.

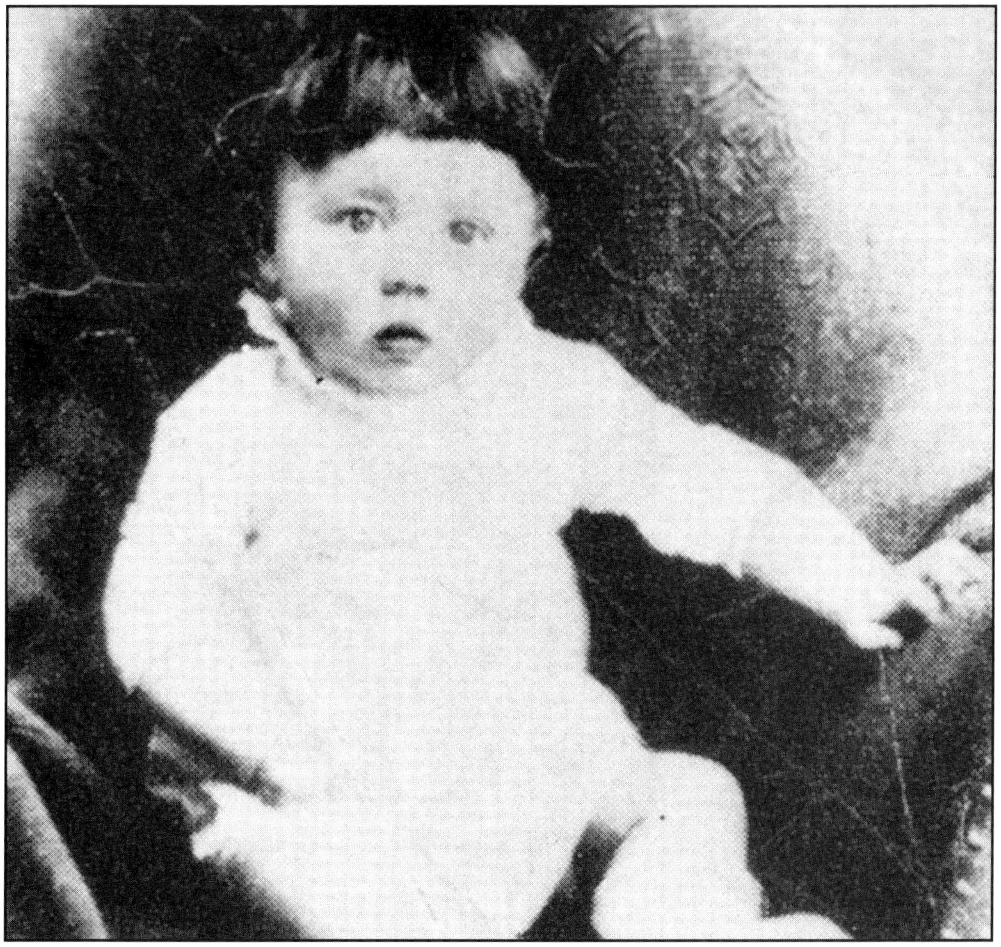

LEFT: A rare picture of Adolf as a child. Of his four siblings, only his sister Paula survived infancy.

BELOW: Top of the heap – Hitler at school. Goebbels later claimed that Hitler had "led all the playground games".

Left: Germans singing in the Odeon Square, Munich. Hitler (inset) can be seen joining in.

Right: The grave of Hitler's parents. This picture was taken while Hitler was on his way to annexe Austria.

Much has been made of Hitler's development into a power-hungry dictator being caused by a lack of love and affection from his parents. In fact, while his birth may have been humble by the standards of the times, his upbringing was normal, lower middle class. There is no evidence to substantiate the stories later put out by his propaganda chief Josef Goebbels that he frequently had to collect his drunken father from the local inn. Hitler evidently disliked his ever-critical father, possibly the more so for realising that the criticism was often justified.

There is no reason to believe that Alois, stiff and formal as might be expected of a civil servant in the Austro–Hungarian Empire, did not love his son. But it was his mother, Klara, whom the boy adored. She gave him the affection his father did not. In short, she spoilt her son so much that he always expected to have things his own way. The harsh realities of life turned this spoilt child into a vicious, cruel dictator.

Hitler's upbringing was conservative. His prejudices were likewise: he had a hatred of inherited privilege and a tendency to blame foreign (especially Jewish) plots for the shortcomings of his own country.

Left: German officials honour Adolf Hitler in 1936 with a hand-written copy of his book *Mein Kampf*.

Right: Adolf Hitler at Kiel, 1933. He is addressing a parade of Brown Shirts, who totalled 600,000 in Germany.

At school Hitler was an able pupil, although too lazy to continue for long in any project. According to the myth spun by Goebbels, Hitler the schoolboy led all the playground games, being a natural leader and "understanding the meaning of history". (This was the man who ignored the lessons of Napoleon's disastrous campaign and invaded Russia.) In fact the young Adolf was a dreamer who made few friends.

Hitler's father died in 1903 and the family moved to Linz. Here the adolescent Hitler decided he was an artist but, as ever, any inherent talent was wasted by his lack of effort. In 1907 he failed to get into the Vienna Academy of Fine Arts. Within a year his mother died and he was able to live off his father's state pension by claiming to be in full-time education. It was not the only fraudulent claim he was to make.

By 1913 he had despaired of finding the success that always seemed to elude him in Vienna. It was partly for this reason that he decided to move on to Munich. More pressing, however, was his imminent call-up into the Austrian army. He was eventually arrested by the German police and sent home to report for his medical. Ironically, he was rejected on health grounds. At this stage he had few political ideas, but he certainly subscribed to the contemporary vogue of anti-Semitism, which was prevalent in Germany and Austria throughout Hitler's youth – and which was to become the basis of his later credo.

ABOVE: President von Hindenburg ordered the disbanding of Hitler's fascist army. This picture shows how little notice has been taken.

LEFT: Saluting crowds greet Hitler on his election as Chancellor and President, 1933.

HITLER'S CHILDHOOD

Although an able pupil, as a boy Hitler never found the energy or the sense of purpose to make the most of his talents.

In Mein Kampf *– Hitler's credo and political life story – he wrote of an orphaned youth of seventeen, "forced to go far from home to earn his bread". The reality is very different: he lived quite comfortably off his widowed mother for several years. At school he failed so many exams that he was refused promotion to the next grade several times. After his father's death, his indulgent mother could not force the boy to remain at school, and in 1905 he left, having again failed to win promotion.*

Immediately he declared that he would have nothing to do with menial occupations. As an artist, he felt he should be stepping onto a higher plane. And thanks to his mother's adequate pension, he was able to live idly in Linz, where he was to be seen carefully dressed and sporting an ivory-tipped cane, attending the theatre or strolling the fashionable streets.

Lacking any real occupation, he found instead a preoccupation with the inconsequential. He spent hours creating designs of a rebuilt Linz. He took piano lessons and then gave them up. He bought a lottery ticket and dreamed of a future of artistic leisure. When he did not win, he first denounced the lottery organisation, then the cheating government.

A picture by Hitler of the Parliament and Ringstrasse, Vienna. Hitler's pretensions as an artist were never quite matched by his ability.

Hitler succumbed to the grandiose music of Richard Wagner and was so stirred after a performance of Rienzi that while walking with his sole boyhood friend, August Kubizek, he started to declaim about his future and that of his people. When he met Kubizek again 30 years later, he remarked: "It began with that hour."

A dazzling new world opened up to this wayward dreamer when he went to Vienna. Here he discovered nationalism as a prime force in a multi-ethnic city humming with intrigue as the old Austro–Hungarian system started to break up. The ruling Germans had become a minority as the empire stretched into Czechoslovakia and the Balkans. Racism was rife, and focused itself in particular on Jews, whose emancipation in Austria had encouraged an influx of immigrants from Hungary and the East. Between 1850 and 1910, the Jewish immigrant presence in Vienna had risen from 2 per cent of the population to 8.5 per cent.

In this turbulent environment Hitler was to spend six unhappy years, still supported by his mother. His ambition received a blow when his sample drawing for entry into the Academy of Art was rejected. The school's director advised him to try architecture, but he had not passed his final exams at school, which were a prerequisite for entry.

Top right: A sketch by Hitler from his war years. This is the church of Ardoye in Flanders, executed in 1917.

Bottom right: Watercolour by Corporal Hitler. Ruins from World War I fighting.

Below: *An Old Courtyard in Munich* (1914) by Hitler. Hitler later started his "Beer Hall" putsch in this city.

While in Vienna, he was joined by his old friend Kubizek, who was studying music at the conservatory. The two shared an apartment, but while Kubizek worked hard at his studies, Hitler seemed content to continue his aimless course. He sketched, he composed pamphlets attacking landlords, he tried to write an opera and a play. He painted, too, but was rejected a second time when he again tried to enter the academy.

Hitler abruptly left the apartment he shared with Kubizek and rented a room by himself. Nearby was a shop that sold various periodicals including one edited by a defrocked monk who called himself Jorg Lanz von Liebenfels. This magazine, Ostara, *carried headlines such as: "Are You Blond? Then You Are A Creator And Preserver Of Civilisation." It presented a world of Teutonic blonds forever beset by people of mixed race. It advocated castration, selective breeding, programmes of sterilisation, deportation of "undesirables" and liquidation by forced labour and murder. These ideas played a large part in Hitler's later beliefs.*

In 1909 Hitler gave up his room and passed through several addresses. He slept on park benches until the winter forced him to seek shelter in a men's hostel. Here he found one friend, a vagabond called Reinhold Hanisch. The pair teamed up and Hanisch actually sold a number of Hitler's pictures. Finally they quarrelled over a picture of the Vienna Parliament building, which the artist felt was worth 50 crowns but which Hanisch had sold for only 10.

In 1938, when he was in a position to do so, Hitler had Hanisch tracked down and murdered.

RIGHT: The Karlskirche, Vienna, by Hitler. The sketch is a drawing in pencil and watercolour.

BELOW: ***A Ravine Near Ypres*** **(1914) by Hitler. This is a ravine at Wytschaete where Hitler saved his commanding officer's life.**

WAR AND PEACE

WHEN World War I broke out, Hitler petitioned the Kaiser to allow him to join a German regiment even though he was an Austrian. Within a week he had been enrolled in the 16th Bavarian Regiment, his medical problems evidently overlooked. In the army his life was to change. Here he finally found the discipline he may subconsciously have longed for. Though he remained a loner, he also found the equivalent of a family. At any rate, he was essentially happy and he served with honour and distinction as a courier on the killing fields of Flanders.

LEFT: The fiery orator at work – the Führer always held his audiences spellbound.

LEFT: The tenth anniversary of the "Beer Hall" putsch. Survivors of the putsch re-enacted the events of 1923.

BELOW: The marriage of Dr Josef Goebbels. Hitler was a witness for the union.

Left: Hitler's country estate, Berchtesgaden, Bavaria. He spent many days here planning his domination of Europe.

Right: Goering and the Führer at Goering's hunting lodge at Karinhall near Berlin.

Hitler served at Ypres and was always prepared to take on dangerous missions. He won the Iron Cross Second Class which was later converted to First Class – a rare honour for an enlisted man. The Iron Cross, awarded on the recommendation of the regiment's Jewish adjutant, stood him in good stead later when he needed to obtain acceptance as a German.

Army life also helped crystallise Hitler's political beliefs. He said later that he did not think of the war in the same terms as other soldiers – getting through a battle unharmed and finding somewhere warm to sleep – but rather as a general or a politician, examining the grand scope of a military thrust and bewailing the "enemy within". These, in his eyes, were the pacifists, profiteers and Communists, whom he saw as more dangerous than the range of forces mobilised against Germany.

At the end of the war, Hitler was in hospital as a consequence of a British gas attack on his position. Defeat was a bitter pill to swallow, and he could see only one reason for it: the Fatherland had been betrayed, not just by the Marxists and Jews, but also by the politicians.

LEFT: A photograph of Hitler and a small girl. The picture is from the Führer's private album.

TOP RIGHT: Hitler addresses members of his cabinet in 1936. The Nazis polled 99 per cent of the vote. Hess is on the left.

BOTTOM RIGHT: Hitler inspects the Guard of Honour outside the Reichstag, 1936.

Defeat brought terrible consequences to Germany. The Treaty of Versailles that was imposed on the subjugated nation demanded harsh war reparations, which left an impoverished Germany seemingly without hope. In addition, territory had to be ceded and the Rhineland was demilitarised. The army was limited to 100,000 men and, even worse for the collective German ego, insulting assumptions were made that Germany should admit sole guilt for the war and hand over key officers to the victors as war criminals. Not surprisingly, disaffection of one kind or another became widespread.

For the most part, this found its outlet in the spread of Communism, which had succeeded in overthrowing the established order in Russia. Following the 1917 October Revolution, Marxist ideology and egalitarian principles had spread throughout the defeated nations.

Left: The Berlin Olympics, 1936. The German leader refused to congratulate the black athlete Jesse Owens on winning four gold medals.

Right: The Führer speaks to 60,000 of the Hitler Youth at a Nuremberg rally.

The drift to Bolshevism, however, was not without its strident opposition. A strong sense of nationalism first found a voice in the coffee houses and bourgeois clubs, which were the breeding ground of political parties and groupings. Hitler, already noted by various right-wing army officers for his anti-Bolshevist views, became their semi-official mouthpiece, addressing and reporting on the nationalist groups.

In September 1919 he attended a meeting of the German Workers' Party, a 40-strong group that purported to attack both business cartels and trade union tyranny. Its leader, Anton Drexler, declared the party to be a classless, socialist organisation, to be led only by "German leaders". National Socialism had begun.

At the September meeting, Hitler was inspired to get up and speak. His words impressed Drexler so much that he was invited to join the party's committee. It was while addressing a party meeting in this capacity two months later that he made the most significant discovery of his life. He had the gift of oratory. And he had what he had subconsciously craved – an audience for whom he was a messiah.

Hitler enthusiastically organised the party, taking it over completely. He changed its name to the Nationalsozialistische Deutsche Arbeiter-Partei (National Socialist German Workers' Party) and developed a programme offering land reform, abolition of ground rent and various other anti-capitalist notions. He also discovered the secret of propaganda – the more half-baked the idea, the louder you have to shout it.

Stealing an idea from the Communists, he sent lorries packed with uniformed supporters around the streets. They bullied people into supporting Hitler's cause – his first public meeting in 1920 attracted 2000 people. Soon his brown uniformed ex-army supporters were replaced by semi-terrorist thugs sporting his new party emblem, the swastika. Meanwhile, he consolidated his grip on the party. He acquired (probably with money secretly donated from army funds) the local newspaper, the *Münchener Beobachter*, and relaunched it as the *Völkischer Beobachter* (the People's Witness).

As his fame spread outside Munich, important new allies were joining him. Among these were Ernst Röhm, Rudolf Hess, Alfred Rosenberg and Julius Streicher. But his greatest triumph at the time was to recruit air ace Hermann Goering, the last commandant of Baron Von Richthofen's "flying circus" and a national hero. All these disparate characters held extreme nationalistic views; but they had one principal characteristic in common – a vitriolic hatred of Jews.

In 1921 Hitler began to spread his message of hate in Berlin, where he found a ready group of listeners among those who were sickened by the decadence into which the capital had sunk.

His uniformed thugs became the highly-organised SA (Sturm Abteilung, or Storm Troopers) and they were to be seen all over Bavaria beating up political opponents, ripping down rival election posters and openly collecting cash for the "massacre of the Jews". Any heckler who dared oppose a party speaker at a meeting was soon surrounded by Brown Shirts and severely beaten for his pains.

At last the government acted. When the SA disrupted a rival political meeting and assaulted its speaker, Hitler, now officially known in the party as the Führer, was sentenced to three months in jail. He served four weeks and was released a martyr and something of a folk hero to his followers.

But if the chaos after the war had been the launching pad for a fascist party ostensibly offering order, it was a twin stroke of fortune for Hitler that propelled the NSDAP into the forefront of national politics.

First, Germany could not pay the war reparations imposed in the Treaty of Versailles and, when she defaulted, France occupied the Ruhr, the heartland of German industry. This in turn contributed massively to the rampant inflation which spiralled out of control through the early twenties, creating poverty and bitterness among the hitherto affluent middle classes.

In 1923 Hitler launched what was to become known as the "Beer Hall" putsch. At a packed meeting in Munich's Burgerbrau Keller, a beer hall, he declared the Bavarian government had been overthrown, and set off with his private army to march on Berlin, just as Benito Mussolini ("Il Duce" to his followers) had marched on Rome. Hitler's followers, however, got no further than the centre of Munich before they were arrested by the police. The Führer found himself facing a six-year jail term.

In prison, he was treated like a celebrity and he used his time there to write *Mein Kampf* (My Struggle), his credo and vision for an imperial Germany (the "Thousand Year Reich"), most of which was dictated over several years to his faithful deputy Rudolph Hess. When he was released in 1924, Germany's fortunes had changed again. The French were withdrawing from the Ruhr, inflation was being controlled and the NSDAP had been routed at the polls.

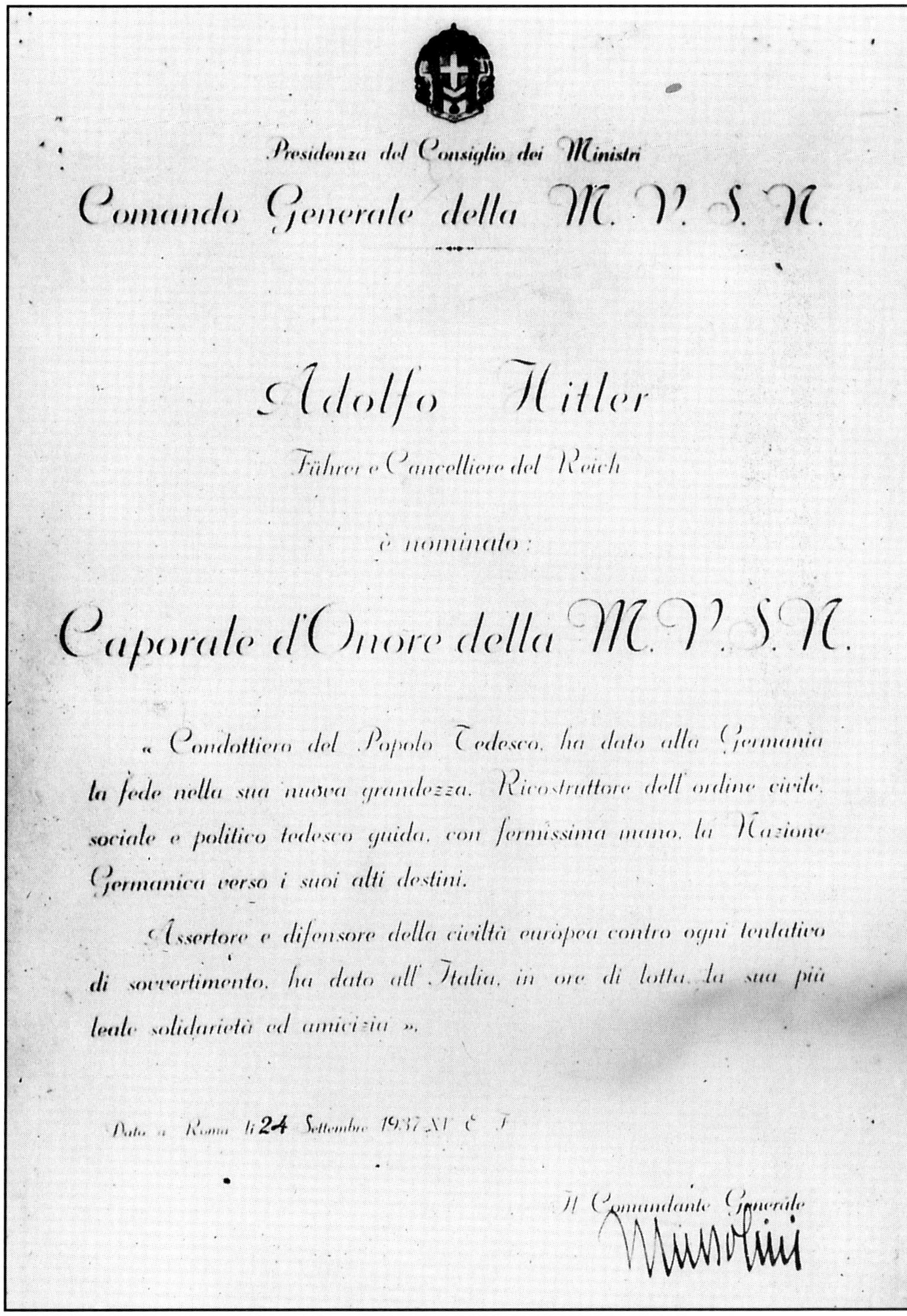

Presidenza del Consiglio dei Ministri

Comando Generale della M. V. S. N.

Adolfo Hitler

Führer e Cancelliere del Reich

è nominato:

Caporale d'Onore della M. V. S. N.

« Condottiero del Popolo Tedesco, ha dato alla Germania la fede nella sua nuova grandezza. Ricostruttore dell'ordine civile, sociale e politico tedesco guida, con fermissima mano, la Nazione Germanica verso i suoi alti destini.

Assertore e difensore della civiltà europea contro ogni tentativo di sovvertimento, ha dato all'Italia, in ore di lotta, la sua più leale solidarietà ed amicizia ».

Dato a Roma li 24 Settembre 1937 XV E. F.

Il Comandante Generale

Mussolini

LEFT: A certificate declaring Hitler an Honorary Corporal of the Fascist Militia in 1937. It was awarded by Mussolini – the only other person who held this post.

OPPOSITE: Hitler's signature.

A new approach was needed. Hitler adapted accordingly, becoming a "democrat". But at the same time he strengthened and reorganised the SA, still under the leadership of Röhm, whose real loyalty was with the regular army. Partly because of this, Hitler created his own bodyguard, the SS (Schutz Staffeln, or Protection Squads), which were to be mobilised so effectively when in 1929 they came under the control of a club-footed failed novelist called Heinrich Himmler. Hitler then successfully quelled a revolt by certain NDSAP branches, who wanted to return to the socialist aspects of National Socialism. So successful was he in doing this that one leader, Josef Goebbels, joined with the Führer and was sent as gauleiter (district leader) to clean up the particularly mutinous Berlin branch of the party. It was the start of the march to power.

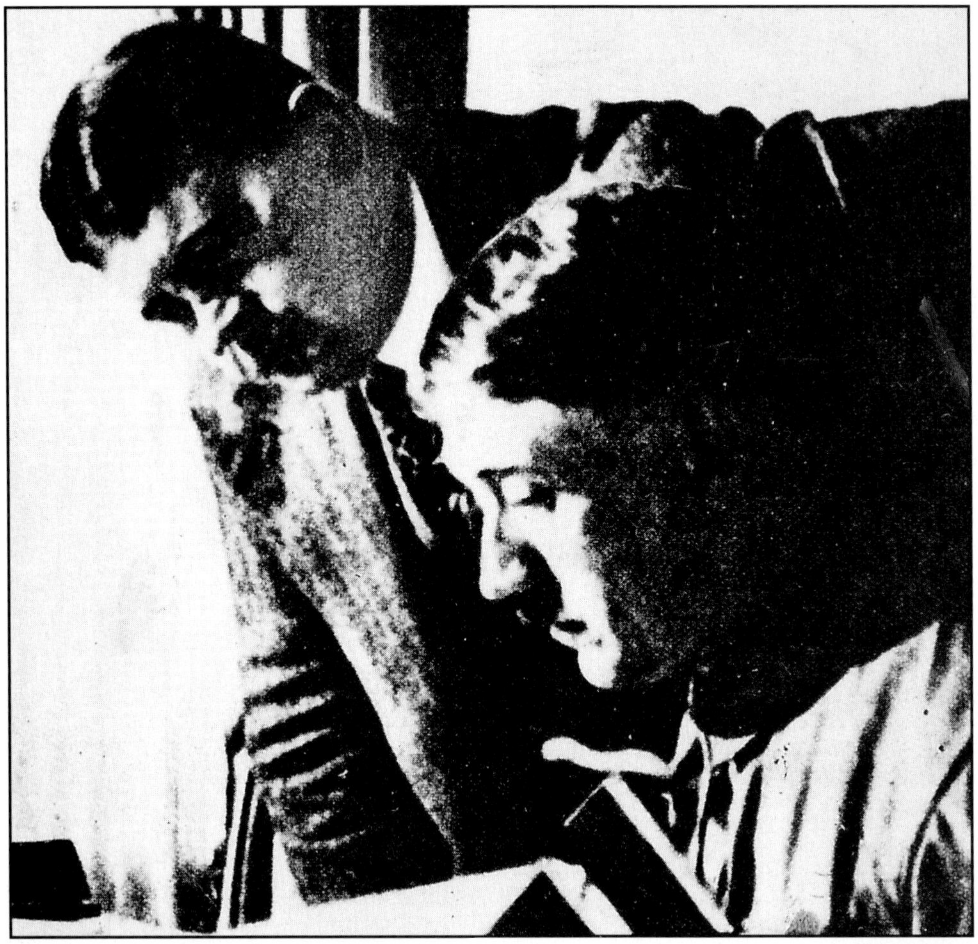

Ernst Röhm and Adolf Hitler in 1934. Hitler later had Röhm murdered in the Night of the Long Knives.

Hitler's double. A man resembling the Führer caused vast confusion at Vienna Zoo when officials were unsure whether to salute him!

HITLER'S HENCHMEN

From left to right, Goebbels, Himmler, Hess and Hitler at a concert in 1933.

Josef GOEBBELS (1897-1945): Small, weak and slightly crippled in childhood by polio, Goebbels was the antithesis of the Aryan ideal. Joined the National Socialists as a Berlin socialist but was won over to Hitler's view and purged his Berlin branch of left-wing elements. Membership doubled under his leadership. Created propaganda chief 1926; organised street brawls and later mass rallies. Propaganda Minister in 1933, he set up Crystal Night, the first mass action against the Jews, and the burning of books by Jewish or Communist authors. Mobilised Germany for "total war" in 1943. Committed suicide soon after Hitler – after first poisoning his six children and shooting his wife.

Heinrich HIMMLER (1900-45): Joined Nazis in 1923 and took part in the Beer Hall putsch. Given control of SS in 1929, he became Berlin police chief in 1933, later head of all German police. Responsible for the "Germanisation" of Poland (the mass murder and transportation of the Poles); subsequently put in charge of Hitler's Final Solution (the genocide of the Jews). Ran concentration camps until November 1944, when he ordered their destruction. Tried to make a peace deal with the Allies. Later caught by the British but swallowed cyanide before he could go on trial as a war criminal.

Reinhard HEIDRICH (1904-42): Himmler's deputy and secret police chief. Organised a fake attack on a radio station near the Polish border by alleged Polish soldiers which served as an excuse for the invasion of Poland. Organised the concentration of Austrian, German and Polish Jews into ghettos, led the Einsatzgruppen in Russia and became gauleiter in Czechoslovakia. Assassinated in 1942 by Czech partisans. In reprisal, all adult males in Lidice were murdered and women and children sent to concentration camps. A further 1000 people were sentenced to death by his special courts.

TOP RIGHT: Hitler inspects the German High Seas Fleet at Kiel in 1936.

BOTTOM RIGHT: Hitler's return to Austria. He is welcomed by crowds as he enters Linz, 1938.

BELOW: The Führer surrounded by his favourite stars: Else Elster, Leni Marenbach, Lilian Harvey, Karin Hardt and Dina Grace.

Gneisenau

WH-322

At Thanksgiving a peasant girl runs up to Hitler to demand a dance. The German leader is happy to comply.

Albert SPEER (1905-81): Architect and friend of Hitler, he organised mass rallies with Goebbels. Became Minister of Armaments in 1942 and massively increased war materials production, largely due to slave labour. Later refused to obey Hitler's order to destroy all German industry in the face of the Allied invasion. Sentenced to 20 years' imprisonment at Nuremberg. Released in 1966 and died in 1981 on a visit to Britain.

Erwin ROMMEL (1891-1944): Called the Desert Fox by the British as a tribute to his brilliant generalship in North Africa. He captured Tobruk, but later was defeated at El Alamein. Organised defences in France against D-Day landings, but was on leave when the invasion came. Involved in the July Bomb Plot, he was given the choice of suicide or trial of himself and his family. He chose suicide and was buried with full military honours.

Girls from the German Singing Federation's Festival all reaching up to shake hands with their idol.

Hermann GOERING (1893-1946): World War I fighter ace. Early member of the Nazi party, he founded the Gestapo (secret police). Head of the Luftwaffe. Influence steadily declined after German failure in the Battle of Britain. Committed suicide two hours before his scheduled execution at Nuremberg.

Martin BORMANN (1900-?) Head of party administration and secretary to Hitler. Controlled access to Hitler in his final years. Escaped to South America after the war. Fate unknown.

German motor aces greet Hitler at the opening of the Berlin Motor Show, 1937.

Rudolph HESS (1894-1987): Early party member and assistant in writing Mein Kampf. *Deputy Führer until he parachuted into Scotland in 1941 on a personal peace initiative. Sentenced to life imprisonment, died (believed suicide) in Spandau Jail, Berlin.*

Ernst ROHM (1887-1934): Homosexual head of the SA, remained a rival to Hitler until he was murdered in the Night of the Long Knives.

Gregor STRASSER (1892-1934): Socialist member of the National Socialist party. A serious rival to Hitler, he was murdered in the Night of the Long Knives.

Julius STREICHER (1885-1946): Rabble-rouser and anti-Semitic editor of the racist publication Der Sturmer. *Ousted from party posts in 1940 after insulting Goering. Hanged at Nuremberg.*

Alfred ROSENBERG (1893-1946): Nazi philosopher who developed racial and cultural theories. He had little influence on policy, but was hanged at Nuremberg.

Joachim von RIBBENTROP (1893-1946): Foreign Minister from 1938. Hanged at Nuremberg.

Adolf EICHMANN (1906-62): SS Chief of the Gestapo's Jewish Office. Under Himmler, he was entrusted with carrying out the Final Solution. Escaped to South America, abducted from Argentina by Israeli agents and executed in Jerusalem.

THE MARCH TO POWER

BY 1928 Hitler was a national figure. Though still not taken seriously by the traditional parties, the Nazis nevertheless polled 2.6 per cent of the vote and a dozen Nazi deputies, including Goebbels, took their seats in the Reichstag, the German parliament. The political balance swung in Hitler's favour with the collapse of the New York stock exchange when the rigours of depression hit the world. As Germany's dole queues lengthened to six million, agitators stirred up unrest. The nation's misfortune was blamed, as ever, on the Jews. Party membership soared; after the elections of 1930 the Nazis had 107 deputies, second only to the Social Democrats with 143 and well ahead of the Communists' 77. Germany had become ungovernable democratically, and for several years the Weimar Republic president, war hero Field Marshall von Hindenburg, ruled by decree.

Hitler admires one of the many new building programmes started by the Nazis during the 1930s.

LEFT: The Führer and Il Duce arriving in Munich in festive mood for the Four-Power Conference, 1938.

RIGHT: Professor Albert Speer and Adolf Hitler study maps for the reconstruction of Berlin.

In 1932 Hitler stood against Hindenburg in a presidential election. Mass meetings, torchlight rallies and, for the first time, use of aircraft to carry the Führer to meetings the length and breadth of Germany were organised by propaganda chief Goebbels. Hitler lost to Hindenburg. But he had won 37 per cent of the vote.

This support was translated into seats when elections were called later that year. Hitler's Nazis became the biggest single party in the Reichstag, with 230 deputies. Though they had not got a majority, power seemed a heartbeat away. Hitler, however, refused to deal with the Social Democrats. He was prepared to wait.

The inevitable call came in 1933, and Hitler was made Reich Kanzler, or Chancellor. Even then, he was not considered a serious threat. The older politicians thought they could control him, and must have been increasingly alarmed as he gradually brought every aspect of government under his or his supporters' control. His intentions became clearer when he took measures against his opponents. Already comprehensive, he had the excuse to make them draconian when the Reichstag was burned down. He blamed the Communists and used the event as an excuse to attack them and consolidate his dictatorship.

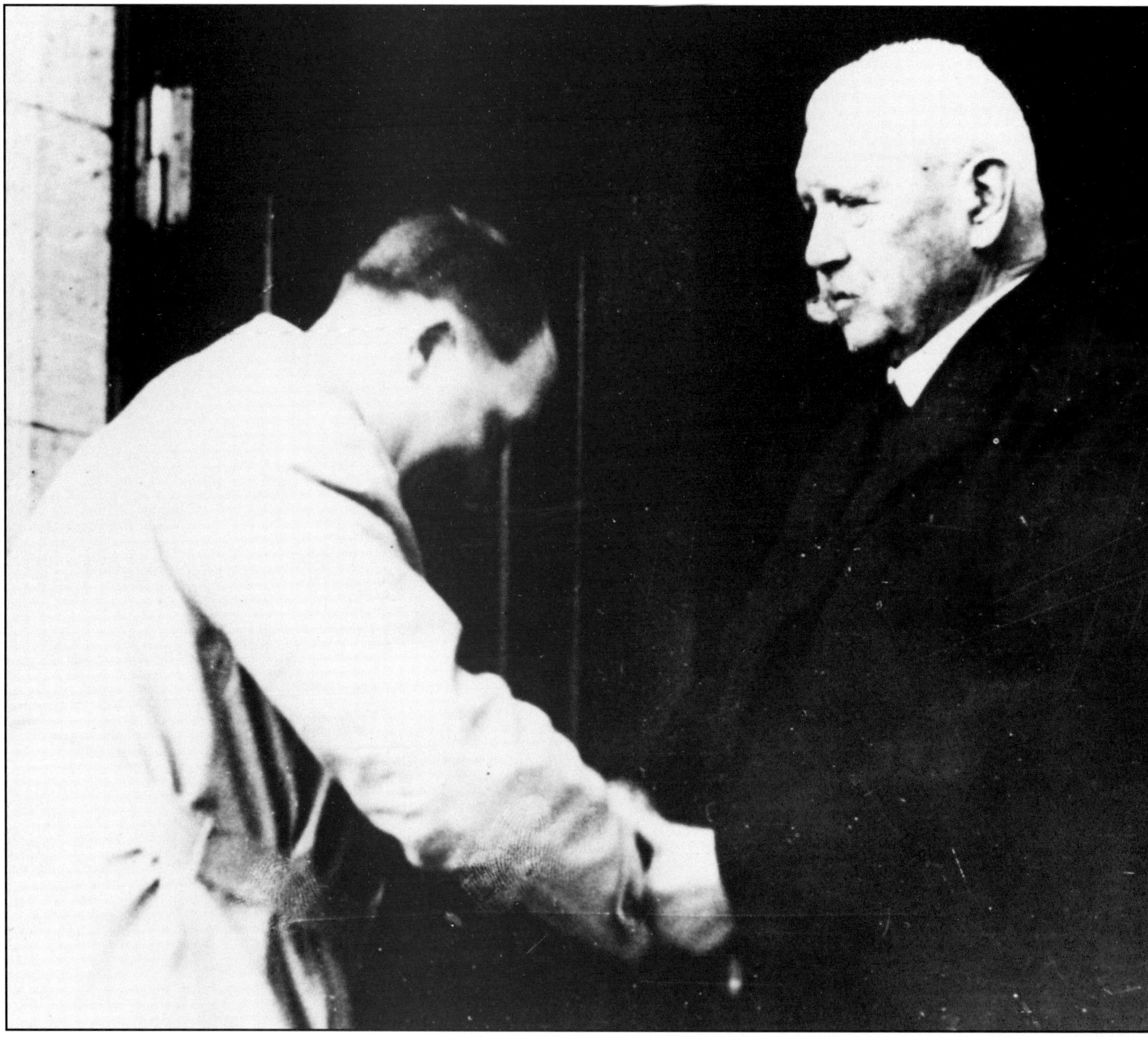

First he increased his parliamentary muscle by outlawing Communism and preventing the party's deputies from taking office. Hitler suspended civil rights, began weeding out Jews from professional jobs and passed an Enabling Bill giving himself virtually unlimited power. His power became absolute with the death of Hindenburg in 1934. Hitler combined the roles of President and Kanzler. He was now unstoppable. He began huge rearmament programmes and even concluded a treaty with Britain that allowed him to increase the size of the navy.

The Treaty of Versailles was torn up, conscription went ahead, communist and anti-fascist books were burned, the first concentration camps were opened and a campaign of terror was launched by Nazi street gangs against political opponents and the Jews – an outpouring of hatred that ended in the infamous Crystal Night when Jewish shops, offices and synagogues were attacked and glass littered the streets of every town.

FAR LEFT: An extremely rare sight – Adolf Hitler bows to President von Hindenburg.

LEFT: In 1938 Chamberlain declared "peace in our time". Less than a year later Great Britain and France declared war on Hitler's Germany.

When Hitler suspected his old ally Röhm and the SA of plotting a second revolution to oust him, he struck against them on the Night of the Long Knives. In the purge, Röhm himself was dragged from bed and executed. All power was now in the hands of the Führer and his henchmen. In his first test of the world's resolve, Hitler marched into the demilitarised zone of the Rhineland. The world did nothing.

In 1936 German forces tasted action when the Condor Legion helped Franco in the Spanish Civil War. More importantly, the German Luftwaffe got its first experience of bombing raids over Spanish cities. In 1938 they marched into an acquiescent Austria. This Anschluss, or annexation, of Hitler's homeland was later accepted in a plebiscite by the Austrian people.

The events of 1938 brought the biggest crisis to face Europe since World War I. Hitler clearly stated that his policy of Lebensraum would culminate in German possession of all lands inhabited by Germanic peoples. His next target was the Sudetenland. After the Sudetenland, Czechoslovakia would undoubtedly follow. British Prime Minister Neville Chamberlain issued a warning that Britain would ally herself to France if Hitler proceeded along his desired course.

Hitler, however, dealt skilfully with the problem. At the Munich conference with Chamberlain, he sent the British leader home with a promise of peace on his infamous "piece of paper" – while the Sudetenland was ceded and Czechoslovakia's fate was sealed.

The subsequent invasion of Czechoslovakia spelled the end of the policy of appeasement. Hitler's word was revealed as worthless and the world awakened at last to his intentions. Britain and France pledged to support the independence of Hitler's next logical target, Poland.

Adolf Hitler and Neville Chamberlain meet. Chamberlain returned home to deliver a false promise of peace.

EVA BRAUN

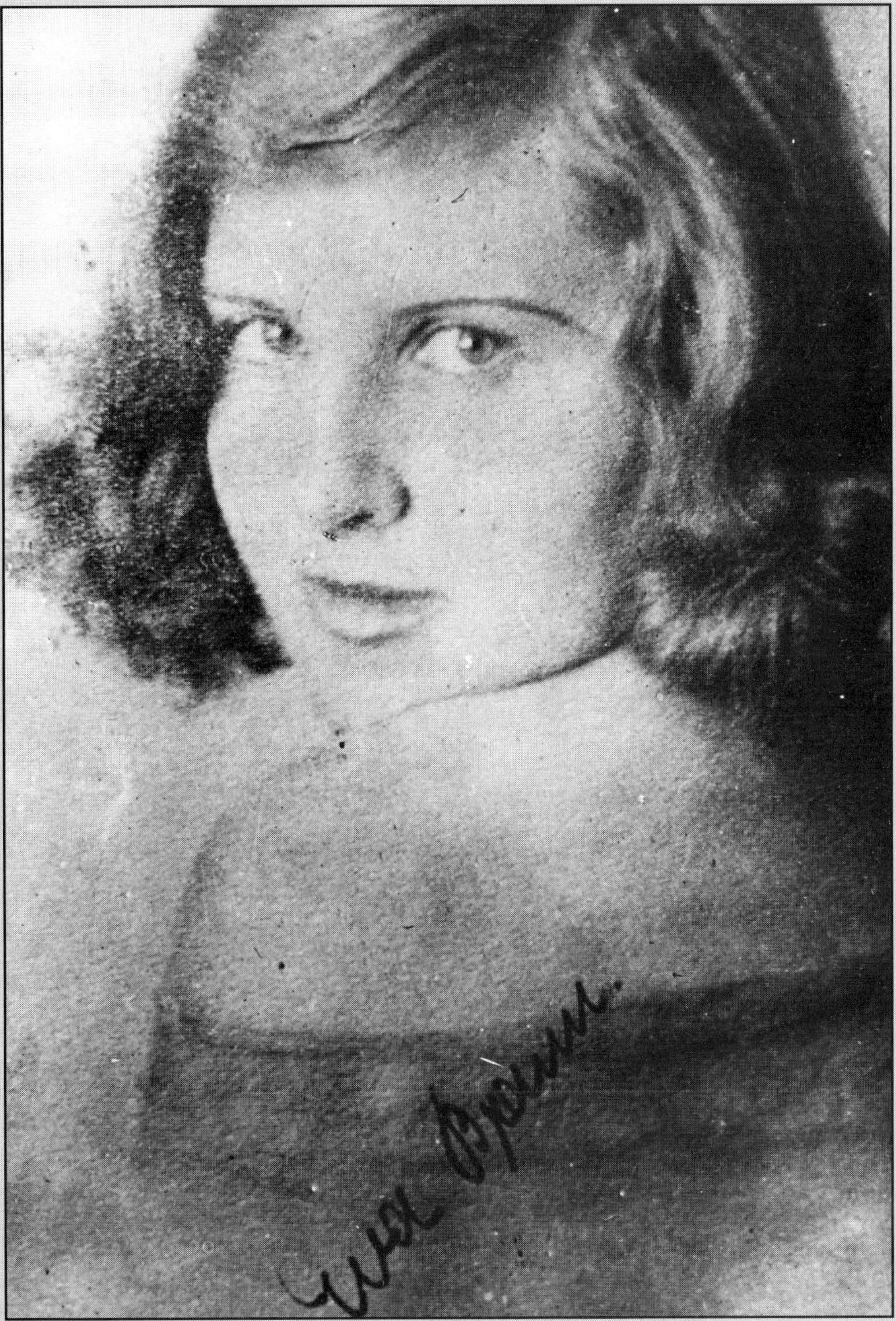

The photograph of Eva Braun that the Führer always carried in his wallet.

If Hitler was spellbinding at his early political meetings and at his later, stage-managed mass rallies (he often stated that these mass audiences were his only bride), he was even more so to the opposite sex.

Why this was so is difficult to discern, possessing as he did a graceless gaucherie that left him stiff and formal at any gathering where people he instinctively recognised as his social superiors were present.

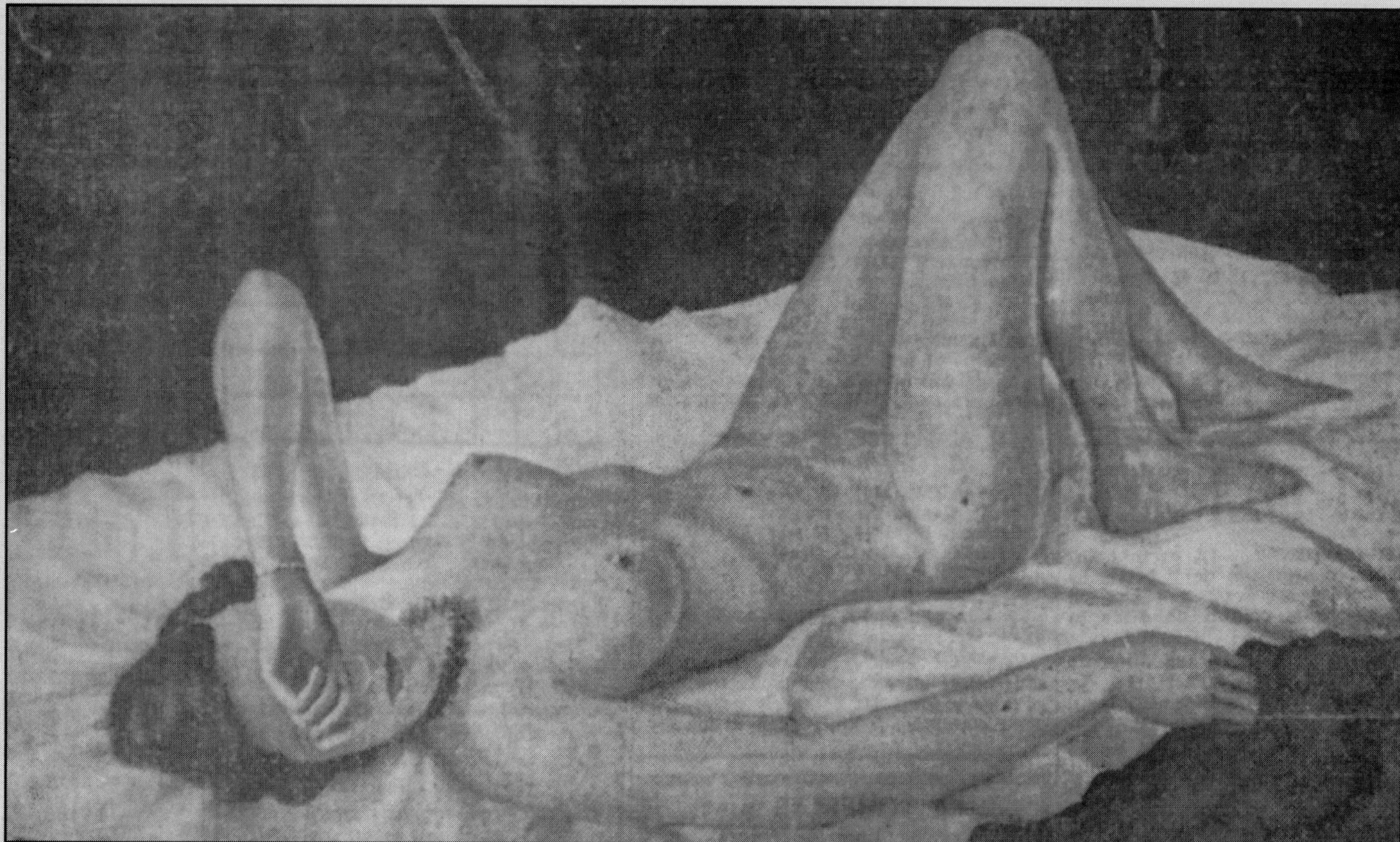

ABOVE: Eva Braun: painted by O.F. Ressel, allegedly from a photograph.

Nonetheless, in the early years the fledgling Nazi party gained much of its influence through women, who were perhaps initially overcome by Hitler's oratory. Many gave, or willed, large sums to the party. Middle-class hostesses, who felt particularly threatened by Communism, vied to have the Führer at their soirées. Little is known, however, about Adolf Hitler's sex life.

As a youth in Linz he had an early passion for a girl whom he saw regularly but to whom he never spoke. His first real relationship is believed to have been with Geli Raubal, the seventeen-year-old daughter of his half-sister Angela.

There were murmurings in the party when, in 1929, Hitler moved into a fashionable Munich house and was quickly joined by his niece, Geli. (Oddly, there is a precedent for incest in his immediate family. His father Alois had taken a sixteen-year-old niece into his home and later made her his mistress.) It is not established beyond doubt that Adolf's relationship with Geli was a sexual one – though he was devastated when she committed suicide in 1931. Detractors say she made this final gesture to escape Hitler's demands on her. Others say she was pregnant by him, and he had ordered her death. A more likely catalyst was the arrival on the scene of Eva Braun.

Hitler met Eva at the end of the twenties, apparently in the photographic studio of Heinrich Hoffman, whose wife had been one of the first society ladies to take Hitler under her wing, earning herself the title of Hitler-Mutti (Hitler's mum).

RIGHT: Eva Braun with Hitler. There is a mysterious baby girl present, sometimes rumoured to be their child.

Eva became Hitler's mistress shortly after Geli's death. He was not good to her. An attractive, simple-hearted girl, whose principal interests were fashion, the theatre and gossip, she was kept in mean circumstances at first and was forbidden to smoke or even to dance or sunbathe.

In her diary, she once noted that she was kept waiting for three hours while Hitler fawned over actress Annie Ondra, buying her flowers and inviting her to dinner. She also commented that Hitler had other affairs, noting sadly that "he was fond of such dimensions".

Eva made two attempts at suicide. In 1932 she shot herself in the neck. A further attempt followed in May 1935, during a period of three months in which Hitler "said not a kind word" to her. Only in 1936, when she replaced Angela Raubal as the housekeeper at Berchtesgaden, did the tension between them relax.

Even then, Eva was kept a secret from the German people, always having to use side entrances and back stairs. She was hardly ever allowed to go to Berlin, and was sent to her room whenever guests arrived. One humiliation came when Hitler told his favourite architect, Albert Speer, in Eva's presence, that "a man of intelligence should take a primitive and stupid woman."

Eventually, however, she became an accepted member of Hitler's intimate parties, though film footage of the two together shows Eva always to be in the kind of high spirits that seemed almost forced. Nonetheless, she was prepared to put up with all Hitler's mood swings – and at the end, unhesitatingly chose death with him.

RIGHT: Hitler was cheered for twenty minutes when he arrived in Innsbruck on his plebiscite tour of Austria. Here he is being welcomed by peasant women of the Tyrol.

BELOW: Both Hitler and Mussolini look slightly taken aback at this semi-nude statue. German Foreign Minister Von Ribbentrop (far left); Count Ciano (far right).

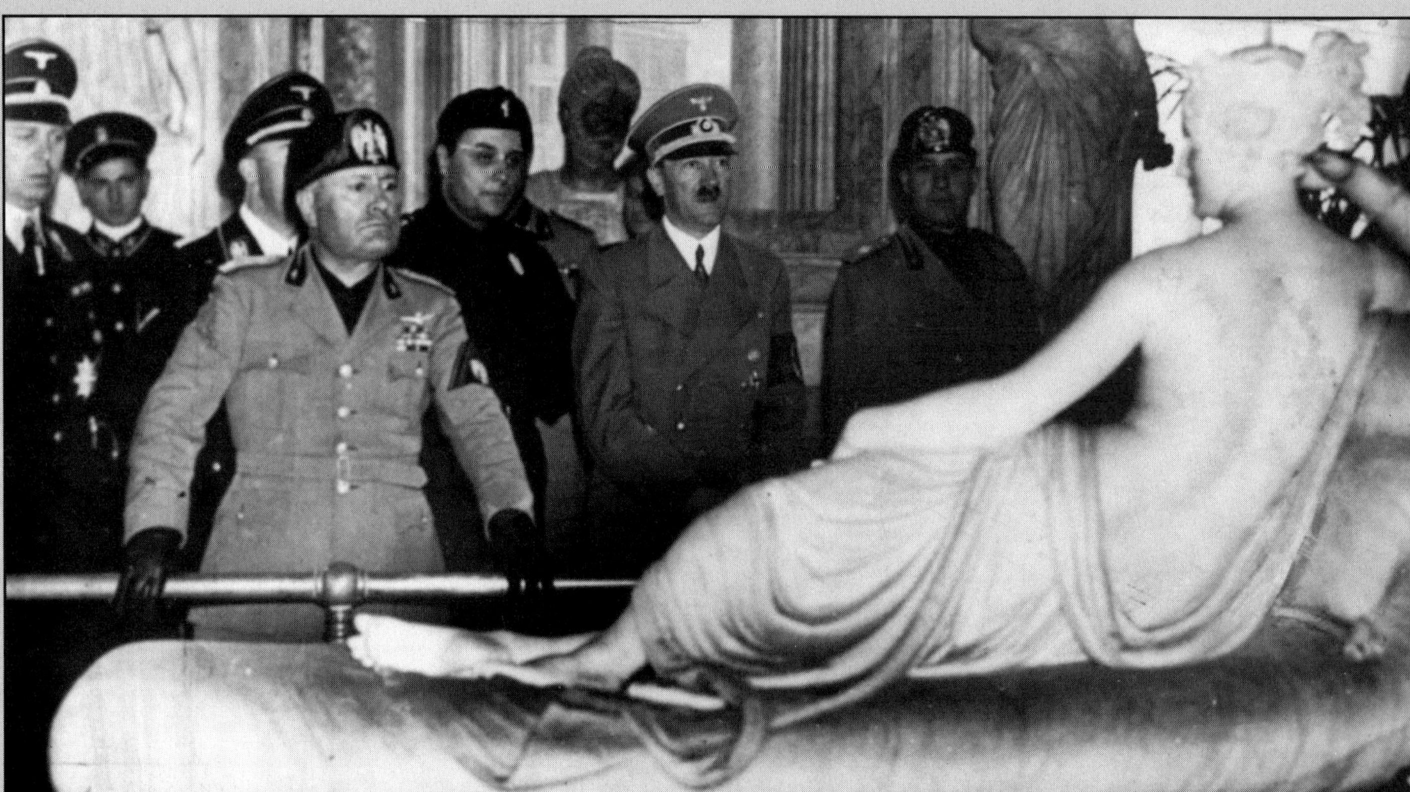

ABOVE: Benito Mussolini, Adolf Hitler and King Victor Emmanuel are saluted by 30,000 troops in Rome, 1938.

LEFT: Hitler in Vienna on the eve of the Austrian plebiscite, 9 April 1938. Rudolf Hess and Josef Goebbels are also pictured.

TOP RIGHT: Hitler, von Hindenburg and Goering at the commemoration of the battle of Tannenberg. Von Hindenburg was the victorious general at Tannenberg in World War I.

BOTTOM RIGHT: Hitler casts his own vote in the Austrian plebiscite in 1938.

Above: Mussolini and Hitler meet in Rome in April 1938.

Left: Hitler at the Colosseum in Rome, 1938.

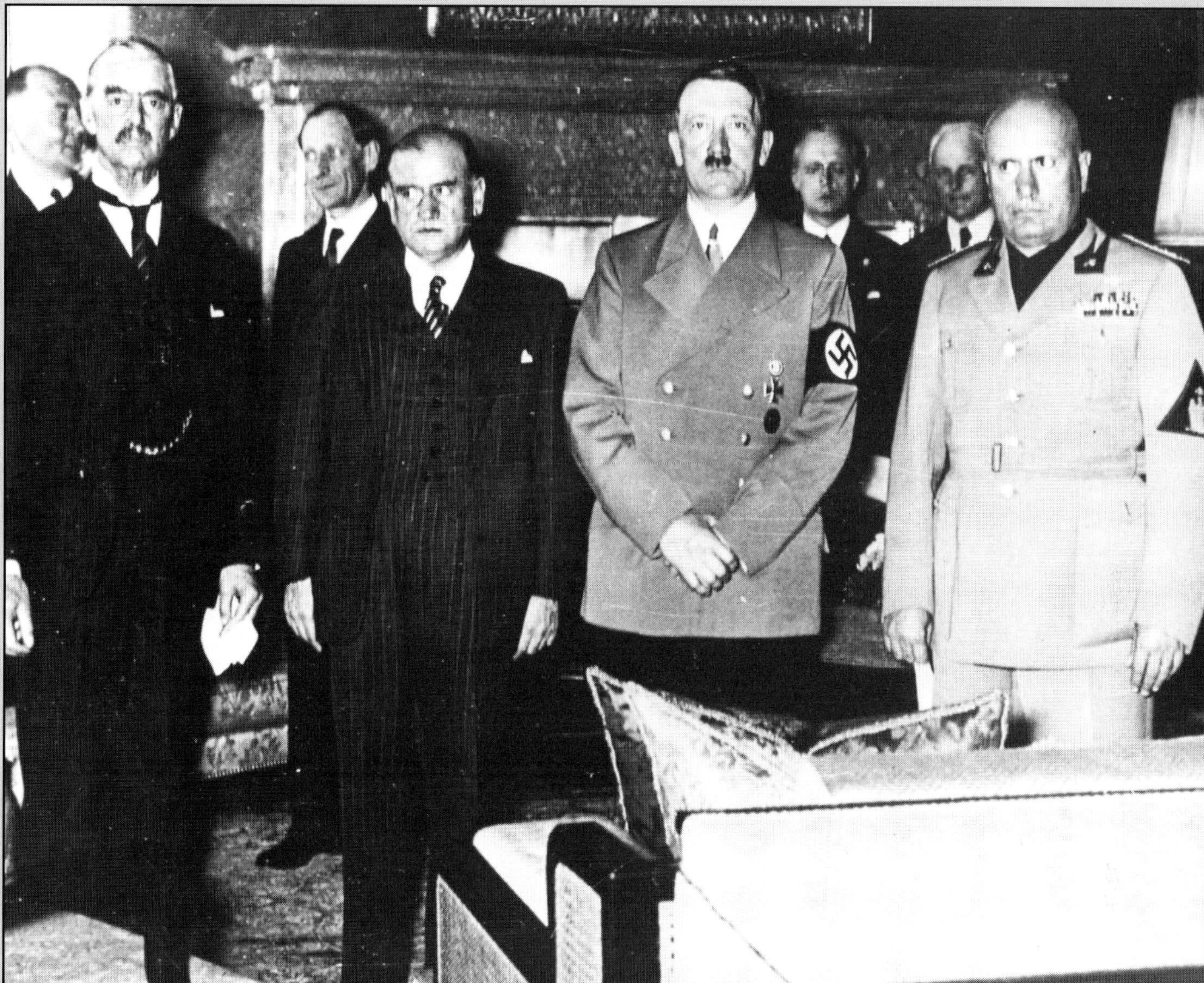

From left to right: Neville Chamberlain, France's Edouard Daladier, Adolf Hitler and Benito Mussolini. In 1938 the "big four" met in Munich to discuss peace in Europe.

The World at War

EMBOLDENED by his success and the weak European stance against him, in August 1939 Hitler signed a non-aggression pact with the newly emerged Soviet Union, which was only founded in 1922. This was more than just an alliance of convenience between two ideological enemies. For Russian leader Josef Stalin, it was the equivalent of Britain's Munich agreement the year before. It bought him time. It also set out spheres of influence that would enable him to take his share of a partitioned Poland, should the Germans decide to invade. For Hitler, it meant one less enemy if Britain and France should fulfil their promises of coming to Poland's aid.

On 1 September 1939 Hitler marched against Poland, and at last Britain and France declared war. The Poles fought heroically, with horse-mounted cavalry charging German tanks, but the invaders managed to crush Polish resistance within four weeks. With the connivance of Moscow, Hitler then partitioned the subjugated country, leaving his eastern borders safe.

FAR LEFT: The German leader inspects fortifications at Engerau, on the Danube. The German army had advanced three miles from the former border at Berg.

LEFT: The population of Memel, Lithuania, salute Hitler in front of their town hall, March 1939.

Hitler had dreamed of an enlarged Europe dominated by Germans, with their racial brothers, the British, running their empire as a second power. For years he had been in contact with Nazi sympathisers in England, and had been encouraged by the growth of Oswald Mosley's fascists. His cause was also bolstered by the apparent sympathies of the former king, Edward VIII, by then the Duke of Windsor following his abdication.

When Hitler realised that his hopes for a pact with Britain would come to nothing, he knew that she would have to be subdued. More pressing, however, was the problem of the French. The non-aggression pact between Germany and the hated Soviet Union had allowed Stalin to take over a substantial part of Poland, while Hitler gained the freedom to concentrate on his western neighbours.

LEFT: General Antonescu, the Rumanian Premier, meets Hitler.

RIGHT: Adolf Hitler's maiden speech in the rebuilt Reichchancellery in Berlin.

France folded as dramatically as it had before the Prussian blitzkrieg in 1870. The mighty Maginot Line, a system of bunkers and forts along France's eastern border, was bypassed by the simple device of invading through Holland and Belgium. The German war machine needed just five days to overrun Holland: Belgium fell in just one.

German tanks poured into France, overrunning vast areas of the country in a mere six weeks. The British attempt to shore up French resistance was ended with the heroic evacuation from Dunkirk. When the German forces turned south to Paris they were opposed by the demoralised remnants of the French army – and total chaos.

Hitler ordered that the French surrender be signed at Compiègne in the same railway carriage in which Germany's capitulation to France had taken place in 1918. He celebrated with a victory parade in Berlin in June 1940, where thousands of soldiers goose-stepped past their Führer.

The seemingly unstoppable Nazis had overwhelmed Poland, Norway, Denmark, Luxembourg, Holland, Belgium and France within the space of three months. And the victories were truly Hitler's, because only he had realised and acted upon the importance of tanks and heavy armour in modern warfare. Only he had conquered the problem of logistics and supply. Only he had made the trains run on time.

Hitler had demanded long-range cannons on his tanks. He had equipped his Stuka dive bombers with banshee, ear-splitting sirens. He had devised the plans for the sudden overthrow of his European neighbours. In due course, Hitler's judgement would once again fail. For now, however, he was the military genius of the age.

BERLIN
MÜNCHEN
WIEN
NÜRNBERG
BRAUNAU
EGER
SAARBRÜCKEN
MEMEL
DER FÜHRER IN SEINER GEBURTSSTADT BRAUNAU 12-3-38
12 + 38
Deutsches Reich
1889
50.
1939
Geburtstag des Führers

LEFT: A postcard celebrating Hitler's 50th birthday.

RIGHT: Hitler makes a speech to the German Parliament shortly after breaking the Danzig and British naval treaties, April 1939.

Even so, he read the signs wrongly. At a Berlin parade to celebrate victory over France, it was as if the war had been won. In fact, it was just starting. Italy now joined Germany, though Mussolini's demands of Nice, Corsica, Tunisia, Djibuti, Syria and Malta angered the Führer. Hitler told him bluntly that the time for such discussions would come only after Britain was out of the war. Finland joined the Germans, though Spain, which had lost 10 per cent of its population during the Civil War, declared itself friendly but neutral.

When Winston Churchill took over as Prime Minister in London and inspired his countrymen with his defiance and determination to fight on, Hitler, alone among the Nazi leadership, realised that defeating Britain in Europe would not be the end of the British war effort. He knew the war would be continued from Canada or some other outpost of a worldwide empire. He could foresee that an English government in exile in Canada would almost certainly succeed in bringing the United States into the war, while the wholesale defeat of the British Empire would benefit no one but Japan and America.

For this reason, although Operation Sea Lion, the invasion plan of Britain, was launched, it was not Hitler's greatest priority. He still sought an alliance. Before he was prepared to attempt an invasion of Britain, he demanded 40 army divisions, a network of heavy artillery all along the French Channel coast and complete mastery of the air.

And so began the Battle of Britain. It was to be, to use Churchill's later words, "if not the beginning of the end, at least the end of the beginning". The Spitfires and Hurricanes of the Royal Air Force, flown heroically by the gallant "Few", narrowly defeated the German Luftwaffe. Britain, for the present, was safe.

Hitler turned again to siege tactics, throwing a ring of steel around the British Isles. By October 1940, Operation Sea Lion had been abandoned. Instead, submarines patrolled the seas to try to starve the enemy into submission. What Hitler needed more than military victory was a treaty with Britain to enable him to pursue his aims eastwards. Always he dreamed of the conquest of the despised Soviet Union. But with Britain still fighting on, there was always the danger of the United States joining the fray.

LEFT: Goebbels always encouraged Hitler to pose for publicity photos. Here the German leader receives flowers from a girl and a boy from the Hitler Youth at the Berlin Automobile Exhibition, 1939.

RIGHT: Hitler's 50th birthday. Vast numbers of tanks, heavy calibre guns, and soldiers parade past the Führer.

Left: The Führer, with plenty of support behind him, shows off his military strength.

Top right: Hitler and the Italian delegation salute on the balcony of the German Parliament after the signing of the Berlin-Rome Axis agreement on 22 May 1939.

Bottom right: The Führer and an Army General consult troop movements on the German-Polish front.

Yet still Hitler emanated an aura of power. Europe was almost his. Fascism reigned supreme. Even Marshall Petain, leader of the collaborating French government based in Vichy, said France had been "morally corrupted by politics". Democracy was in decline.

The decision to attack Russia before the war in the west had been won remains one of Hitler's least comprehensible decisions. Yet there was a certain logic to it.

With Britain under Churchill vowing there would be no peace with Germany, Hitler was becoming concerned by the gradually increasing role of the United States. It was the war he wanted to avoid. So it became urgent to defeat the only army left in Europe to face him: the Red Army. It was vital to remove this obstacle before any full-blooded intervention from across the Atlantic by the world's most powerful nation. At the same time, Stalin was increasing his strength. Hitler had to strike quickly.

Above: Hitler declares war. On 1 September 1939 Hitler announces to the Reichstag that Germany is at war with Poland.

Left: All the Reichstag salute as Hitler makes his speech.

Right: The German leader in animated fashion as he addresses a Nazi rally.

In his fantasies, he saw the rapid defeat of Russia as the final turning point. Not only would there be no European ally left for Britain, the Japanese would be freed from the giant at their rear to begin their southern expansion programme. This in turn would tie up the United States in the Pacific and force Britain to surrender. By sweeping through North Africa, Russia and the Near East, his way would be clear to Afghanistan, from whence he could strike at the jewel of Britain's empire: India.

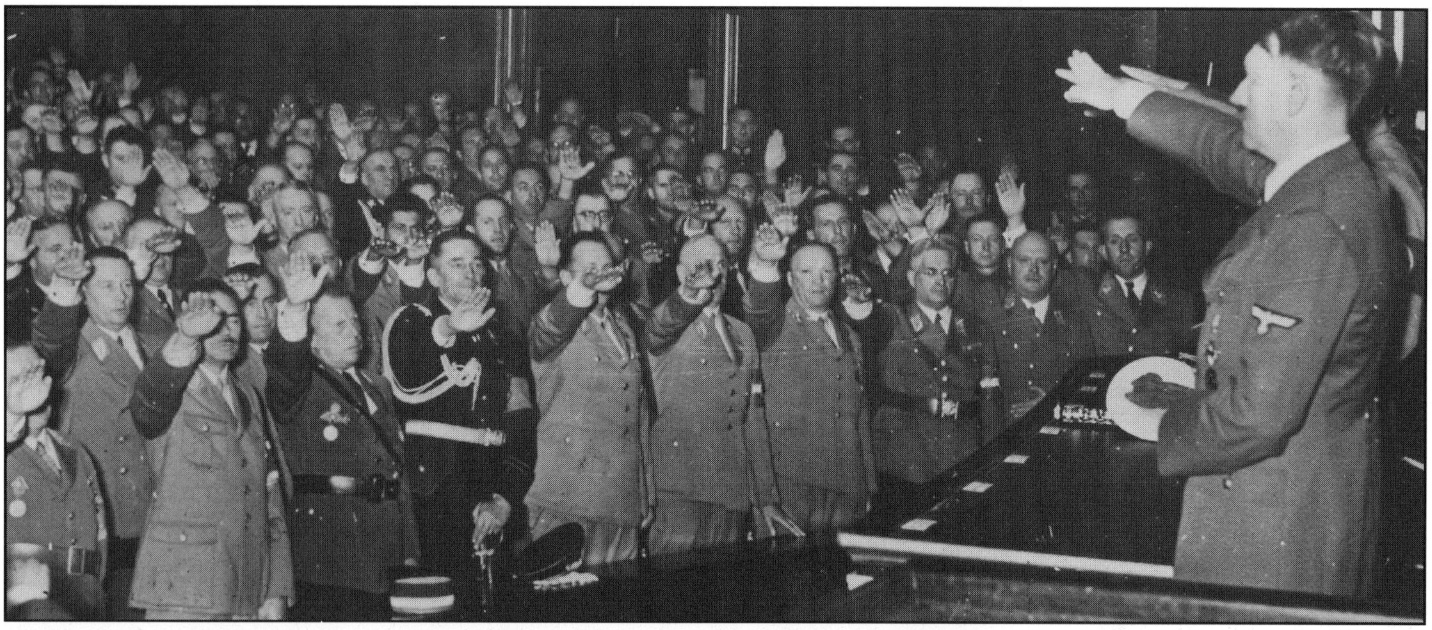

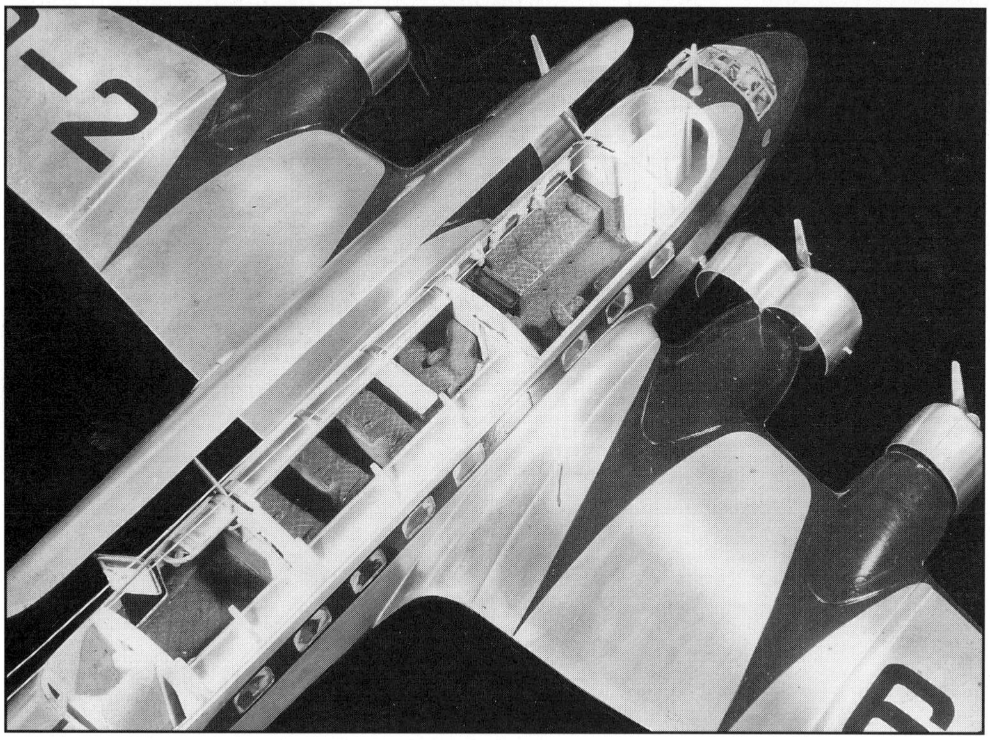

ABOVE: In the Kroll Opera House, Berlin, Hitler tells the world that Germany "will carry on her task alone and that bombs will be met with bombs."

LEFT: A model of the Focke-Wolf "Condor" four-engined plane customised for Hitler's use.

In North Africa, the Nazis and their Italian allies swept through the deserts to gain the hugely important prize of the oilfields. But there was never enough oil to supply the troops scattered across the vastness of Russia. And German industry could not yet supply the 600 tanks a month that would be required to maintain the war effort.

On 22 June 1941 Hitler began his own personal war with Russia. He launched Operation Barbarossa, with 153 divisions, 3580 tanks and 2740 planes against the Bolsheviks. He also launched a new terror. The notorious Einsatzgruppen (special squads) were unleashed with orders to exterminate Jews, gypsies, Asiatics, anti-fascist intellectuals, commissars or anyone capable of becoming a leader. The normal rules of warfare as practised in the west were suspended in Russia. The Final Solution – the annihilation of the Jews – had been extended to include the Russians.

ABOVE: Goering and Hitler discuss tactics.

LEFT: Von Ribbentrop and Hitler at the Berlin Olympics in 1936.

Hitler's Downfall

Left: Il Duce and the Führer look down on Russian territory after a five-day meeting in 1941.

Right: With the threat of an Allied invasion, Hitler surveys his Siegfried Line defences in 1941.

IF the conquest of Russia had an element of logic in its conception, Hitler had ignored the lessons of Napoleon's disastrous campaign. He was aware of the huge empty spaces of the country and the fighting spirit of the Slavs. But he believed Moscow could be taken in six weeks – after which he planned to raze it and create a reservoir in its place.

At first, things went his way. Victory at Kiev included the capture of 650,000 prisoners. But the Russian "scorched earth" policy of destroy and retreat was taking its toll. As the Russians melted away and drew the Wehrmacht ever deeper into the enormous, empty land, a typical German quip was: "No enemy in front of us, no supplies behind us!"

Russian heroics and suffering at Stalingrad are now legendary. But it was at the gates of Moscow that Hitler came to the end of 20 years of unremitting success.

By the autumn of 1942, the Russian campaign was going badly wrong. Stalin had decided the scorched earth policy had gone far enough. There was now a massive German front exposed and a seemingly endless supply of Russian reservists were thrown into the fray.

Hitler's rages directed against his generals could not reverse the decline in the Wehrmacht's fortunes. By April, after a series of bitter battles, German casualties stood at more than a million, or over 31 per cent of the Eastern Army. And they were held just 62 miles from Moscow.

The campaign was demoralising the Führer. Goebbels, visiting his master at headquarters, noted that he was "very much aged . . . serious and subdued". Hitler began to complain that the sight of snow caused him physical pain. On a break in the Bavarian mountains in April, he was caught by a late snowfall. He hurriedly departed. "It's a kind of flight from the snow," Goebbels wrote in his diary, making the ironic link with the winter defeats in the east.

Even with the German advances in the late spring, Hitler's nerves were still unstable. And still he underestimated his opponents' capabilities. He gave the order to entrench in southern Russia, take the eastern oilfields and deny the Russians use of the agricultural lands. Once more his vision was betrayed by his army's incapacity.

Even so, by August 23, the Sixth Army had reached the Volga and Stalingrad.

The conquest of Stalingrad was meaningless in itself, as German troops already controlled the river traffic. Hitler, however, was a man with a mission. Despite the protests of the Chief of Staff, Field Marshall Halder, that he could not sustain campaigns in both the Caucasus and Stalingrad, Hitler gave the order to attack. He fired Field Marshall List when the Caucasus campaign faltered and took command of Army Group A himself. Yet from that moment he became a recluse. He broke off communication with his headquarters staff, and left his Berlin blockhouse only after dark and by concealed routes.

Meanwhile, casualties continued to mount in the house-to-house battle for Stalingrad. His commanders begged him to halt the suicidal attacks. He ignored them. The city had become a matter of prestige.

Hitler was so immersed in his crusade in Russia that he neglected other war fronts. In North Africa, Erwin Rommel's Afrika Korps was bogged down through lack of reserves and supplies. The submarine offensive was failing because Allied ships were better equipped to deal with them. And in the air, the British tactic of blitzing the factories of the Ruhr had been replaced by terror bombing of non-military cities. With the entry of the United States into the war, German cities were suddenly pounded by bomber raids 1000-strong, by day and by night.

LEFT: Hitler and Mussolini with German and Italian generals on a visit to the Russian Front.

FAR LEFT: From left to right: Mussolini, General Jodl, Hitler, and General Keitel study maps at the Russian front in 1941.

BELOW: From left to right: Italian General Cavallero, Mussolini, General Keitel, Hitler, General Jodl, and Major Christian plan their next move against Russia.

At last Churchill was able to talk convincingly about the "end of the beginning". The truth of this was quickly demonstrated on all fronts. On 2 November, Montgomery finally dealt Rommel a crushing blow at El Alamein. A week later Allied troops invaded Morocco and occupied the whole of French North Africa. And 10 days later came the Russian counter-offensive at Stalingrad which led to General Paulus and 220,000 men being surrounded.

Hitler's response was evidence of the state of his mind. When Rommel asked permission to retreat into the desert, he was told to fight on until victory or death. When Paulus reported his predicament, he was ordered to move his headquarters into Stalingrad and throw up a defensive perimeter. Meanwhile, Hitler sent his troops into hitherto unoccupied areas of France.

Instead of preparing for the worst he was reported to have spent his time fantasising about world domination and taking morbid enjoyment from the vast arrays of enemy troops and firepower that he believed were preparing their onslaught for him alone.

By February 1942, the battle for Stalingrad was hopelessly lost and 91,000 German troops fell into Russian hands. Fewer than 10,000 were to return home, years later.

The inevitable result was that Hitler was driven ever closer to the verge of a breakdown. He became increasingly irascible and developed a high degree of hypochondria. In his fantasies, he began to see himself as a modern Macbeth, driven to his destiny by an overbearing fate. He saw himself as a giant going ever more flamboyantly to his doom in a blaze of glory.

LEFT: Hitler with a child. Rumours circulated as to whether Eva Braun might have had a child by Adolf.

FAR LEFT: Hitler and his generals inspect a Paris church shortly after capturing the city.

LEFT: A little girl asks for an autograph.

RIGHT: Hitler meets General Antonescu, the Nazi puppet ruler of Rumania.

And all the time his physician, Theodor Morrell, was dosing him with up to 28 different drugs a day. As the doses became stronger, so too did the sedatives that were needed to calm his jangling nerves.

The state of Hitler's physical and mental health may have had a bearing on his most serious miscalculation. In 1941 he decided to declare war on the United States, though he was still heavily involved on Russian, European and North African fronts.

Why he did so is a mystery. It was the war he most feared. However, his biographer, Joachim C. Fest, put forward a theory to explain this move. Hitler, he said, had long since signed the Tripartite Pact with Japan and had pressed his Far Eastern allies to attack either the Soviet Union or British colonies in South East Asia. When the Japanese attacked Pearl Harbour on 7 December 1941, Hitler was lost in admiration at the audacity of his Nipponese allies, and at their request he declared war four days later.

His reasoning was that the Americans would be largely tied up in the Pacific and he could pursue his submarine war against Britain with greater ferocity by attacking American supply ships. It was also a chance to veil the crisis in Russia and, deep down, a recognition that his war plans had foundered.

Declaring war on the most powerful nation on earth had been another grand gesture. It was also a terrible blunder, the greater as he had already discovered the unreliability of his Italian allies, now spreading his war to Greece, Yugoslavia and soon back to Italy itself.

Britain's island fortress, protected by the Royal Navy and the RAF, could not be taken, and was being supplied from the United States through a special trade agreement. Isolationist America never wanted to join in a European fight, but having been dragged in, all the energy of the New World was poured into the struggle. Allied forces began massing in Britain for the final onslaught.

At the start of the Russian campaign, Hitler was still to be seen at the front from time to time, or else holding rallies. When the defeats began, he lost the energy or the will to strike the poses that he loved. He became prey to melancholia, his left arm trembled permanently and he needed a cane to help him walk. It has been suggested that he suffered from Parkinson's Disease, others blame venereal disease or the strychnine in Dr Morrell's medications. (In civilian life, Morrell had been a specialist in venereal diseases.)

At any rate, his conversation deteriorated into monologue. As he became ever more dependent on Morrell's drugs, his personal secretary, Martin Bormann, was allowed to take over the governance of the Reich – and, in effect, the war, as he controlled every audience with Hitler.

Like an old man, Hitler harked back to the past: to Vienna, to the Great War, to his plans for a New Order. He had spies working in the ranks of his own armies and was suspicious of anything new. He took little interest in jet engine development except to order that jets should be used only on bombers, not on fighters. He was never able to grasp the importance of the splitting of the atom or radar. Meanwhile, German cities were being reduced to rubble.

Final defeat in Russia – at Moscow, Stalingrad and Kursk – left Hitler morose and unwilling to leave the "Wolf's Lair", his HQ in East Prussia. He watched from there the long retreat in the east and in Italy. He waited for a miracle he knew would never come. He continued to think in continents and millennia, clinging on to his dream of an Aryan hierarchical superpower, with Slavic, oriental and black races enslaved and a world free of Jews. He was unable to turn his mind to immediate practicalities.

As defeat loomed, his plans for the New Order became more manic. The killing camps were put into overdrive. He sent out orders concerning the "emigration" of entire races and the "scrapping" of others.

With the opening of a second front in Sicily in July 1943, Mussolini tried to make Hitler see the sense of Italy capitulating to the Allies, leaving Hitler free to defend the line of the Alps. Hitler would have none of it, and with the fall of "Il Duce" on July 25, he decided to occupy Italy.

Opposition within Germany was reaching epidemic proportions. Yet Hitler seemed to bear a charmed life, adding to his feeling that he was a man of destiny.

In the spring of 1943, two bombs planted in Hitler's plane failed to go off. A suicide bomb plot, organised for an occasion when Hitler would be examining new uniforms failed because an allied air raid had destroyed the uniforms the day before. Another bomb went off prematurely and another suicide mission failed when the plotter was refused admittance to a conference. Even Himmler tried to reach a secret accord with the Allies.

On 6 June 1944 the greatest armada ever assembled left the south coast of Britain to strike at Normandy in Northern France. As the Allies secured the beach-heads and advanced on Caen and Paris, a long-time opponent of Hitler decided it was time to strike.

Left: A peasant family poses with Hitler in East Prussia.

Right: Hitler poses for a propaganda photograph with three children.

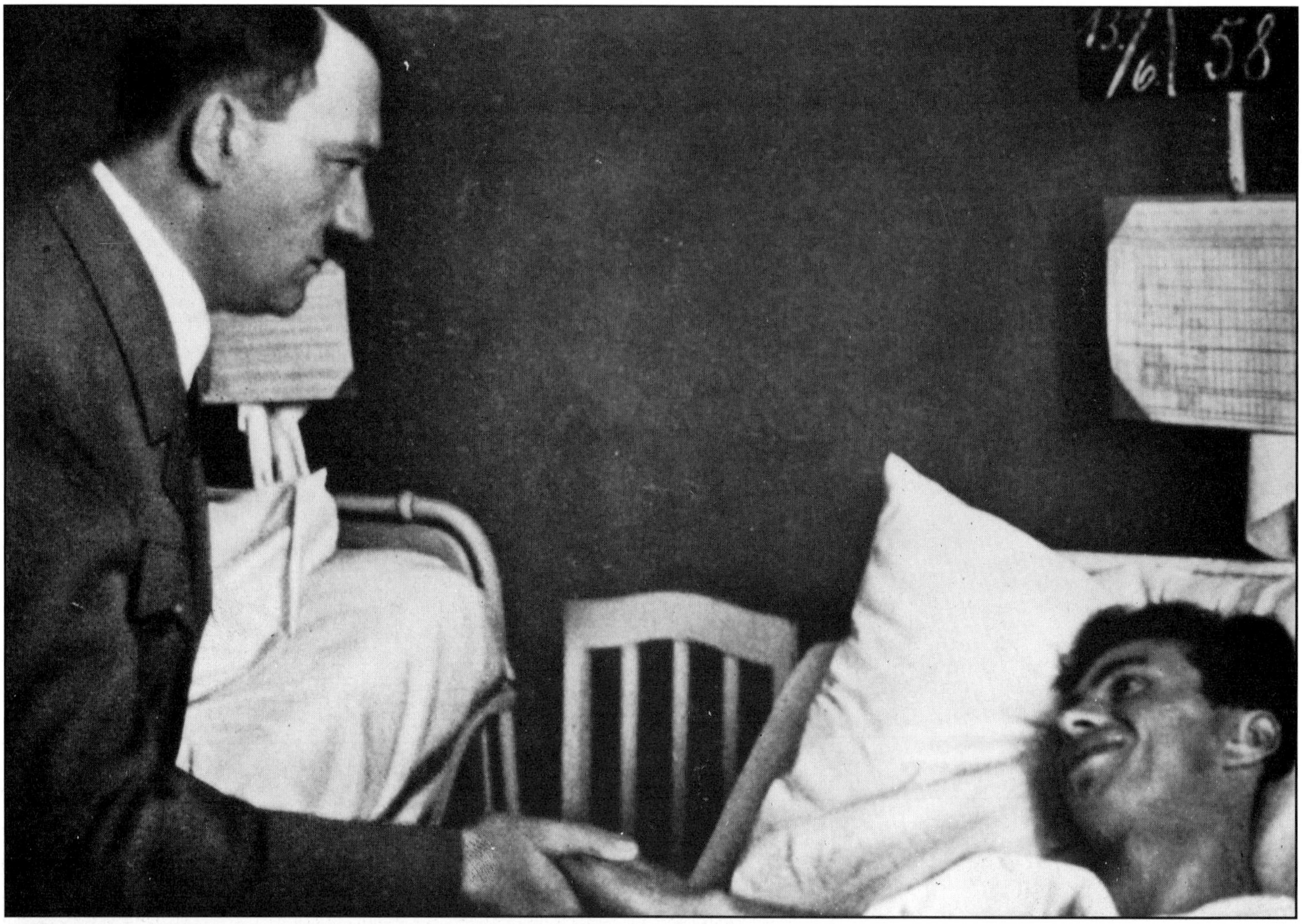

Above: Adolf Hitler visits wounded soldiers in Reinsdorf hospital in 1942.

Left: Hitler smiles while his armed guard (top left of picture) shows the true face of fascism.

Right: The Führer explains the Nazi doctrine to a young boy.

On 20 July Colonel Count Claus Schenk von Stauffenberg, a 37-year-old crippled war hero of North Africa, aided to some extent by his old Commander-in-Chief Rommel, now inspector of defences in northern France, placed a bomb under a table at the Wolf's Lair.

Left: Hitler on holiday in Berchtesgaden.

Right: Holiday time – Hitler strolls through the mountains near Berchtesgaden.

At the last minute, Hitler moved away from the table – and survived the explosion with only cuts and bruises. His revenge was terrible. Hundreds of suspects were rounded up, drummed out of the army and sentenced to death. The order was that they should be hanged – as slowly as possible. Film of the hangings were presented to Hitler, who watched every last twitch with evident gratification. He further declared that every member of the plotters' families were equally guilty; children as young as three and uncles as old as eighty-five were arrested. Rommel himself was given the choice of suicide or death for all his family. He chose suicide. The executions continued until April 1945.

The failed plot had one other effect on Hitler. Following discussions with Mussolini, now reinstalled as a puppet dictator, he placed Himmler in total command of army reserves and made Goebbels the "Minister for Total War". "It takes a bomb under his backside to make Hitler see reason," Goebbels noted in his diary.

Thus began the final effort. Albert Speer's organisational genius saw to it that aircraft production was stepped up to its highest level of the war. Yet at the same time, Allied bombing of refineries and Russian advances across the Rumanian oilfields denied the Luftwaffe the fuel to fly. Hitler's army was still nine million strong, but was spread from Scandinavia to the Balkans. The advancing Red Army was encircling and capturing division after division of troops.

Finland withdrew from the war in August, freeing more Russian troops for the German front and British troops took Athens. Allied forces controlled northern France as far as the Moselle. On 11 September an American patrol crossed into Germany for the first time. Although a Russian thrust into East Prussia was beaten back, the war had come home to Germany.

At the same time, Hitler's health deteriorated even further. He never left his Berlin bunker again, except once to visit the troops in the east, where his generals were shocked by his ghastly appearance. Soon he began complaining of constant headaches and nausea. In September he was laid low by a heart attack.

He was left with two choices: to defend the long frontier to the east and fight off the ideological foe, or to attack in the west. Typically, he chose to attack, in the belief, apparently, that the western allies would tire of the war and join a common cause against Bolshevism.

The Ardennes offensive, the so-called Battle of the Bulge, began in December and was massively successful for a time. Inevitably, however, it was thrown back through lack of supplies and the overwhelming airpower of the Allied forces.

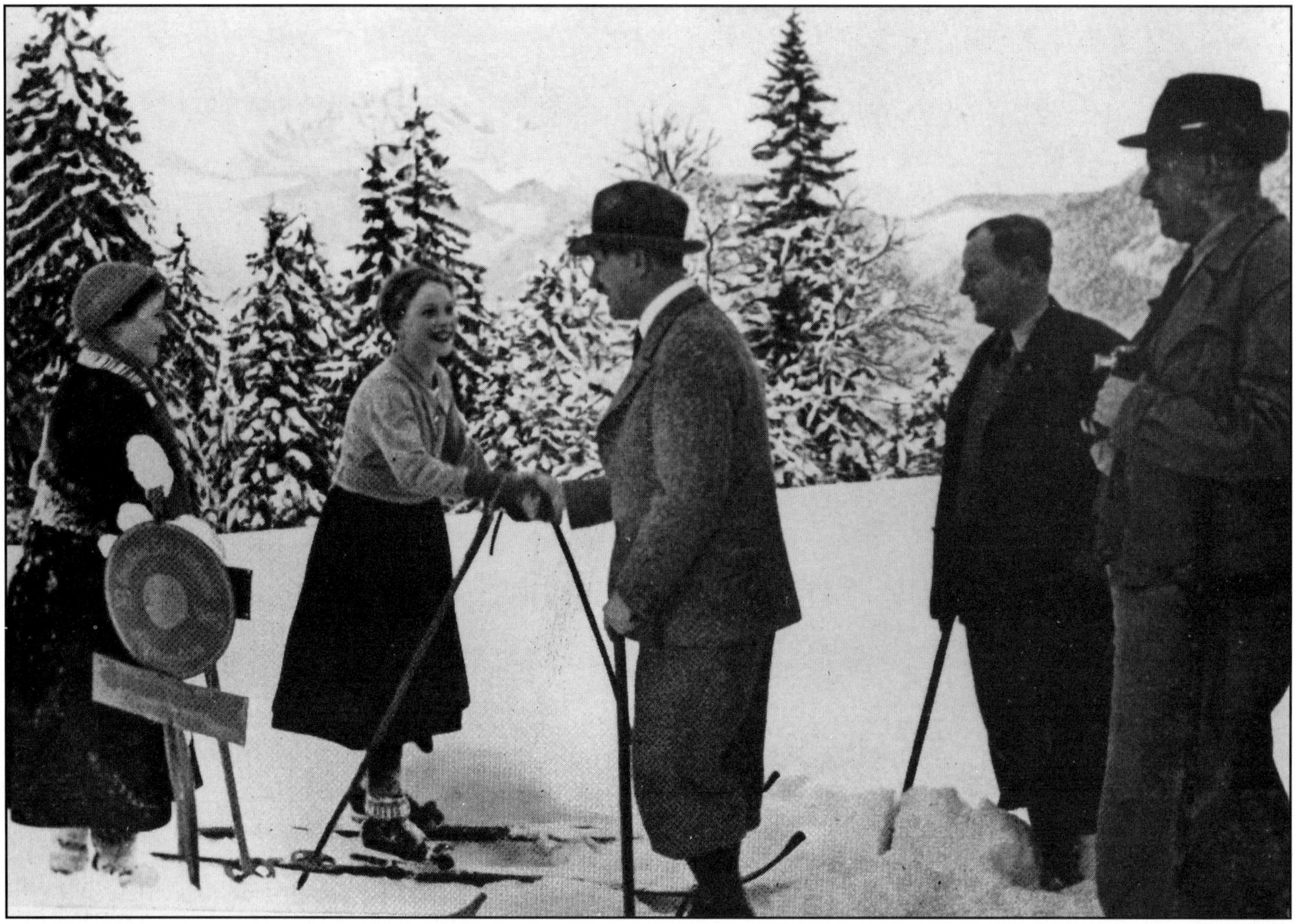

By January 1945, the Russians were 100 miles from Berlin. On 30 January Hitler delivered his last radio address to the German people. Victory would ultimately be theirs, he told them, through their unshakeable will, their sacrifice and their abilities. On the same day Albert Speer sent a note to the Führer telling him the war was lost. Hitler prepared for an end in keeping with the grandiose Wagnerian operas that he loved. His fall would be so dramatic that he would become the stuff of myth and legend, and his desperate ideology would live on.

Children were recruited into the ranks for the last defence of the rubble of Berlin, as Hitler himself remained in his bunker beneath the Reichskanzlerei. Yet there, too, he was no longer safe. For though his authority remained unchallenged until the final hours, even Speer, the man who had come closest to being Hitler's friend, plotted to introduce poison gas into the ventilation system. By another amazing stroke of luck, the system was overhauled the day before the attempt and Hitler escaped yet again.

On 13 April President Roosevelt died. For a time, Hitler was ecstatic. Three days later the Russians launched the final assault on Berlin. On 20 April, Hitler's 56th birthday, Eva Braun joined him in Berlin. All the top Nazis – Goering, Goebbels, Ribbentrop, Himmler, Bormann and Speer – met for the last time and urged the abandonment of Berlin and a final stand at the Berghof in Bavaria. Hitler chose instead to die among the ruins, though he allowed Goering to flee south in the last hours before the capital was encircled.

On 29 April a local magistrate, aptly named Walter Wagner, carried out a civil service of marriage between Hitler and Eva Braun, with Goebbels and Bormann as witnesses. Then Hitler made his will.

ABOVE: Hitler studies a map with typical intensity.

LEFT: Publicity shot of Hitler feeding deer. The Goebbels propaganda machine continually produced such pictures to show Hitler in a favourable light.

FAR LEFT: Hitler takes time off from running the German offensive to go skiing in the Salzburg mountains.

ABOVE: The Führer at home.

LEFT: The Führer enjoys some fruit – he was rumoured to be a vegetarian.

TOP RIGHT: At his eastern headquarters, Hitler examines a map detailing German and Russian losses of 1943.

BOTTOM RIGHT: The Führer tells the Rumanian Premier, Antonescu, how the war is faring in 1943. From right to left: General Keitel, Hitler, Marshall Antonescu and Dr Schmidt.

Even this was largely a polemic against the Jews, though on a personal note he donated his paintings to the town of Linz. Bormann was named his executor, Admiral von Doenitz as his successor and Goebbels, later to commit suicide with all his family when he failed to conclude a pact with the victorious Russians, as head of the government. On the same day, Hitler learned that Mussolini had been shot by partisans on 28 April, along with his mistress Clara Petacci.

LEFT: Hermann Goering explains the difficulties of fighting a war on multiple fronts in 1943.

TOP RIGHT: Assassination attempt – a bomb placed by Colonel Count Schenk exploded just feet from Hitler.

BOTTOM RIGHT: Hitler shows Mussolini the scene of the assassination attempt.

On 30 April Hitler tested the poison he had been given on his beloved dog Blondl, then called his usual military conference. At about 4pm he disappeared into his room with Eva.

According to witnesses in the bunker, a single shot rang out. The commander of his SS guards entered the room and found Hitler slumped over, a pistol in his hand. Beside him was the body of his wife, who had taken poison.

ABOVE: Heinrich Himmler, General Loerser and Mussolini (back to camera) inquire about Hitler's health.

LEFT: Mussolini, overjoyed at the Führer's lucky escape, returns to Italy to fight the Allied forces.

RIGHT: Himmler and Hitler. Allied press speculated that the Führer was concealing an arm injury under his cloak.

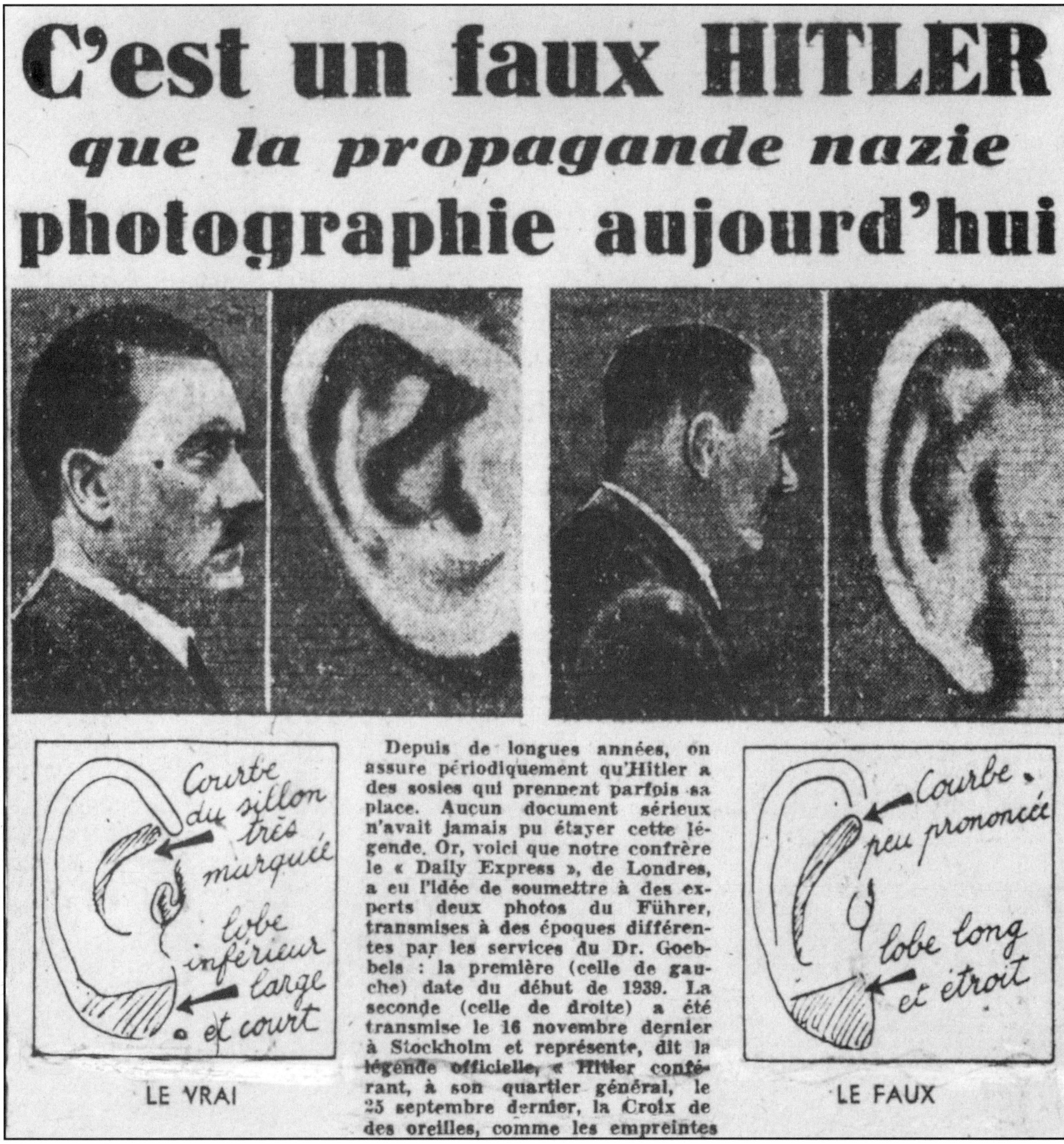

C'est un faux HITLER *que la propagande nazie* photographie aujourd'hui

Depuis de longues années, on assure périodiquement qu'Hitler a des sosies qui prennent parfois sa place. Aucun document sérieux n'avait jamais pu étayer cette légende. Or, voici que notre confrère le « Daily Express », de Londres, a eu l'idée de soumettre à des experts deux photos du Führer, transmises à des époques différentes par les services du Dr. Goebbels : la première (celle de gauche) date du début de 1939. La seconde (celle de droite) a été transmise le 16 novembre dernier à Stockholm et représente, dit la légende officielle, « Hitler conférant, à son quartier général, le 25 septembre dernier, la Croix de des oreilles, comme les empreintes

Press around the world ran stories claiming that the man shown in German propaganda pictures was Hitler's double. Aural experts were asked to give opinions as to whether the man in the photographs was the real Hitler.

Hitler's anniversary speech in 1943. Goebbels and Goering applaud from the front row.

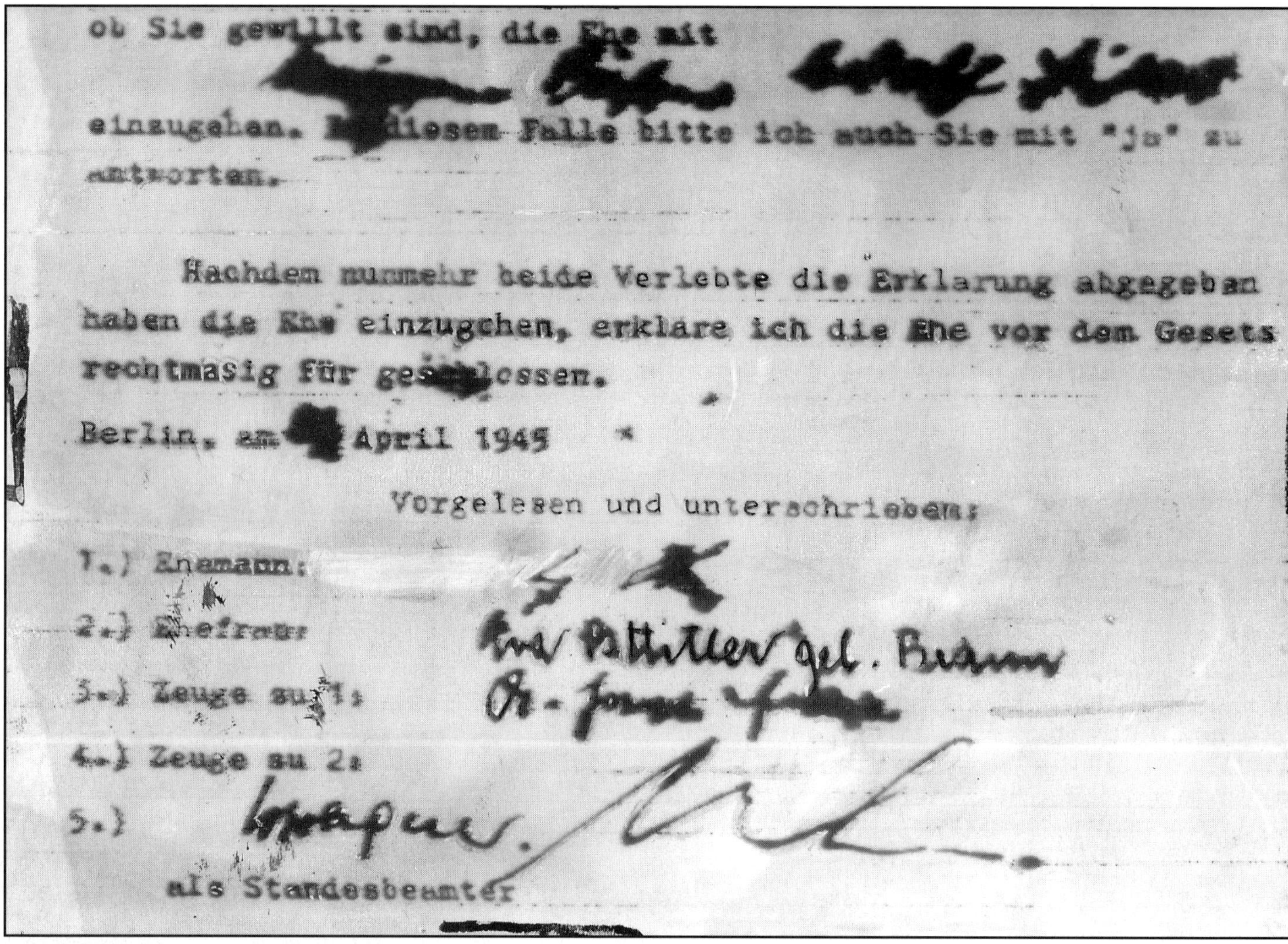

ob Sie gewillt sind, die Ehe mit

[illegible]

einzugehen. [illegible] diesem Falle bitte ich auch Sie mit "ja" zu antworten.

Nachdem nunmehr beide Verlobte die Erklarung abgegeben haben die Ehe einzugehen, erklare ich die Ehe vor dem Gesets rechtmasig für geschlossen.

Berlin, am [illegible] April 1945

Vorgelesen und unterschrieben:

1.) Ehemann:

2.) Ehefrau: Eva Hitler geb. Braun

3.) Zeuge zu 1:

4.) Zeuge zu 2:

5.) Wagner

als Standesbeamter

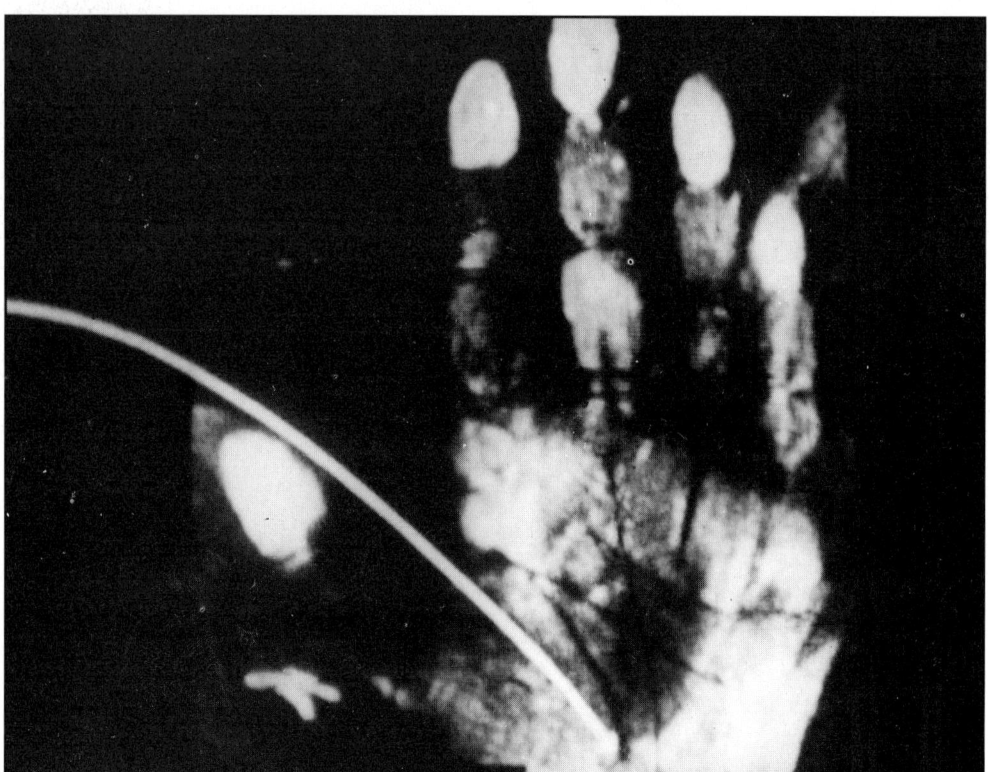

Above: The marriage contract of Adolf Hitler and Eva Braun witnessed by Martin Bormann and Dr Goebbels.

Left: A photograph of Hitler's palm print.

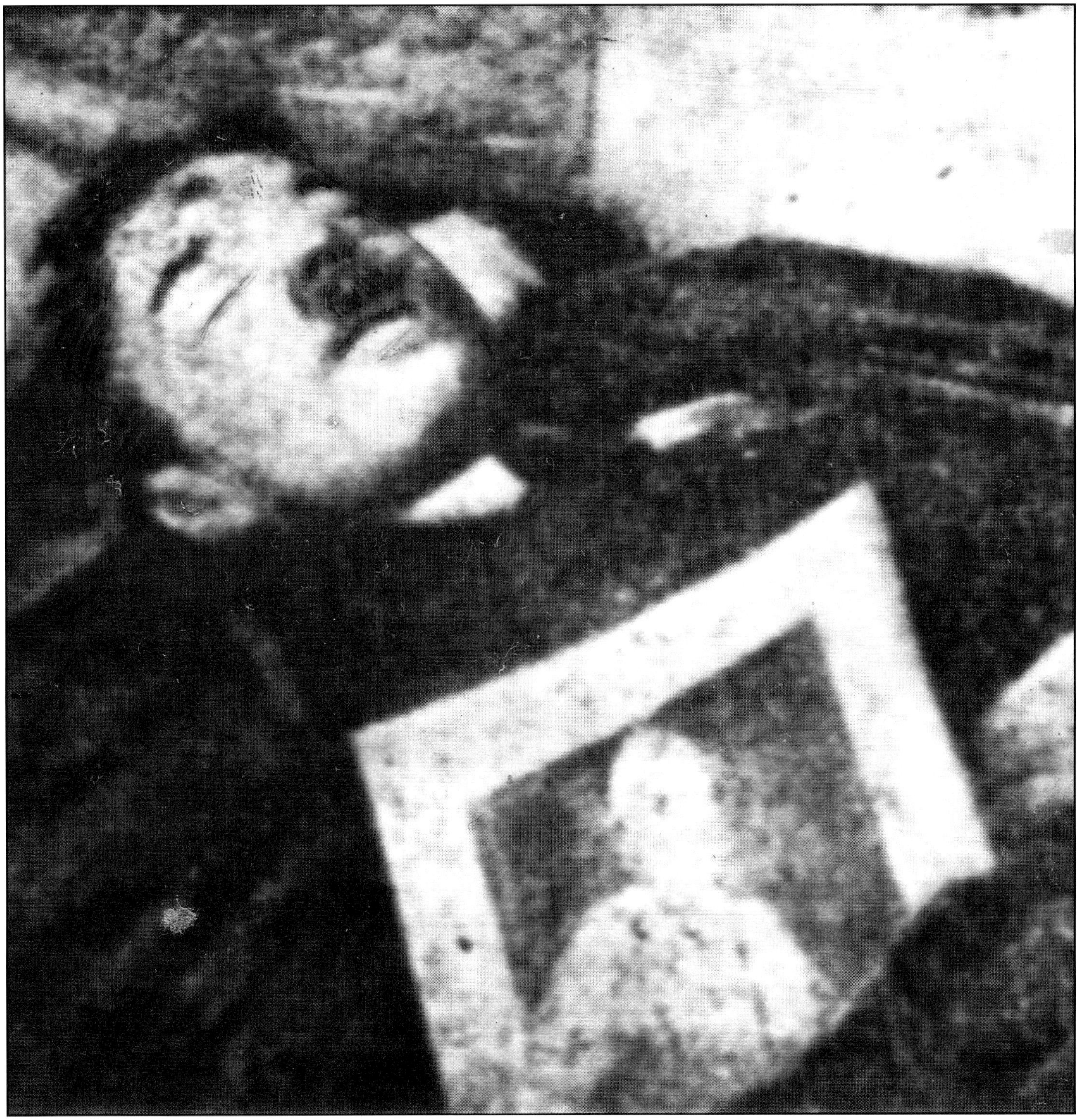

The Russian press released this photograph, claiming it was Hitler. When and where the photograph was taken is still unknown.

Above: Eva Braun's meagre bedroom, in Hitler's Berlin bunker, with a box of poison on the table.

Left: The uniform that Hitler was wearing in the July 1944 bomb plot being burned after the war. It was destroyed to prevent it becoming a "Holy Grail" to Nazis.

Right: Hitler's will was found by Allied soldiers on the capture of Berlin. It is witnessed by Goebbels and Bormann, among others.

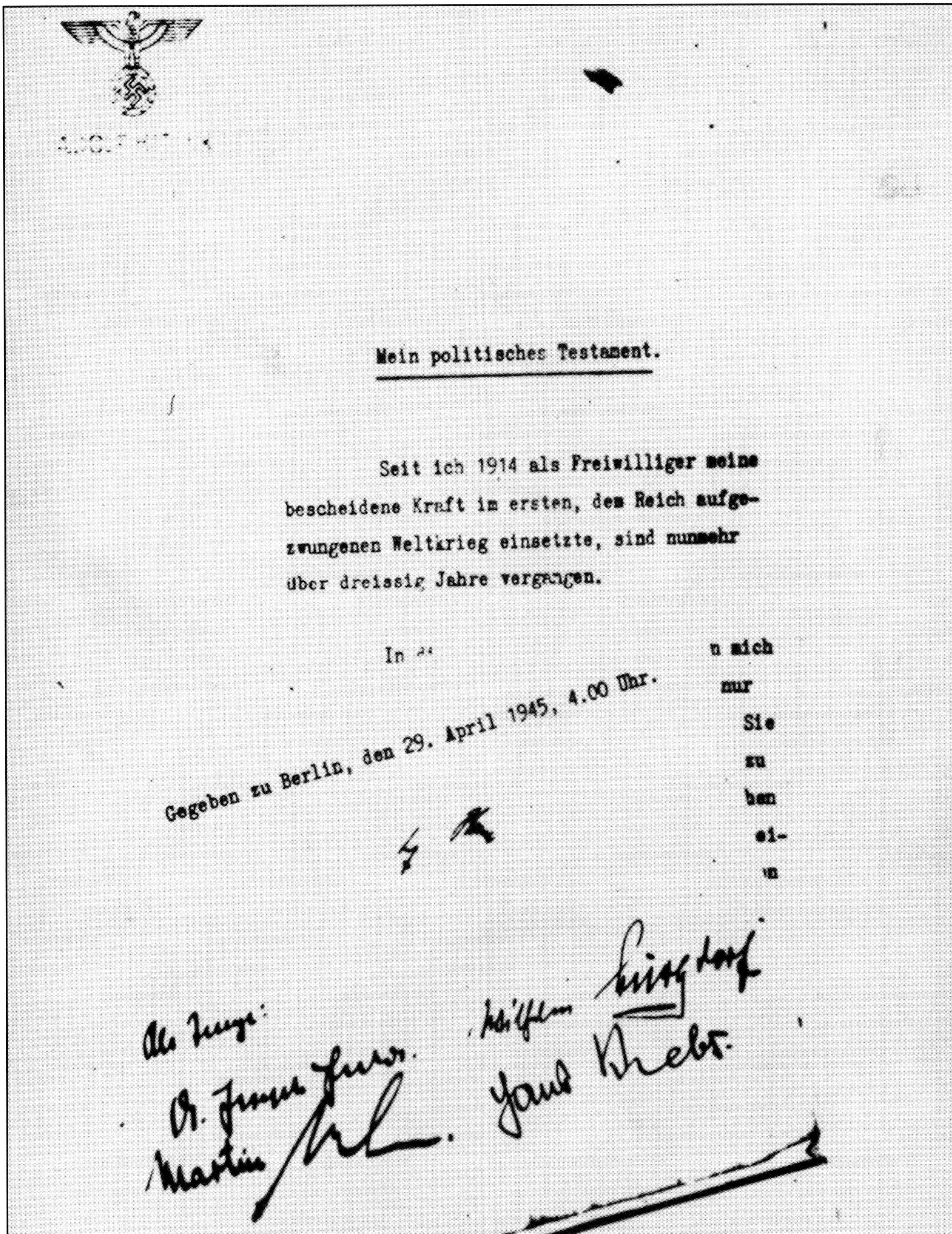

Mein politisches Testament.

Seit ich 1914 als Freiwilliger meine bescheidene Kraft im ersten, dem Reich aufgezwungenen Weltkrieg einsetzte, sind nunmehr über dreissig Jahre vergangen.

Gegeben zu Berlin, den 29. April 1945, 4.00 Uhr.

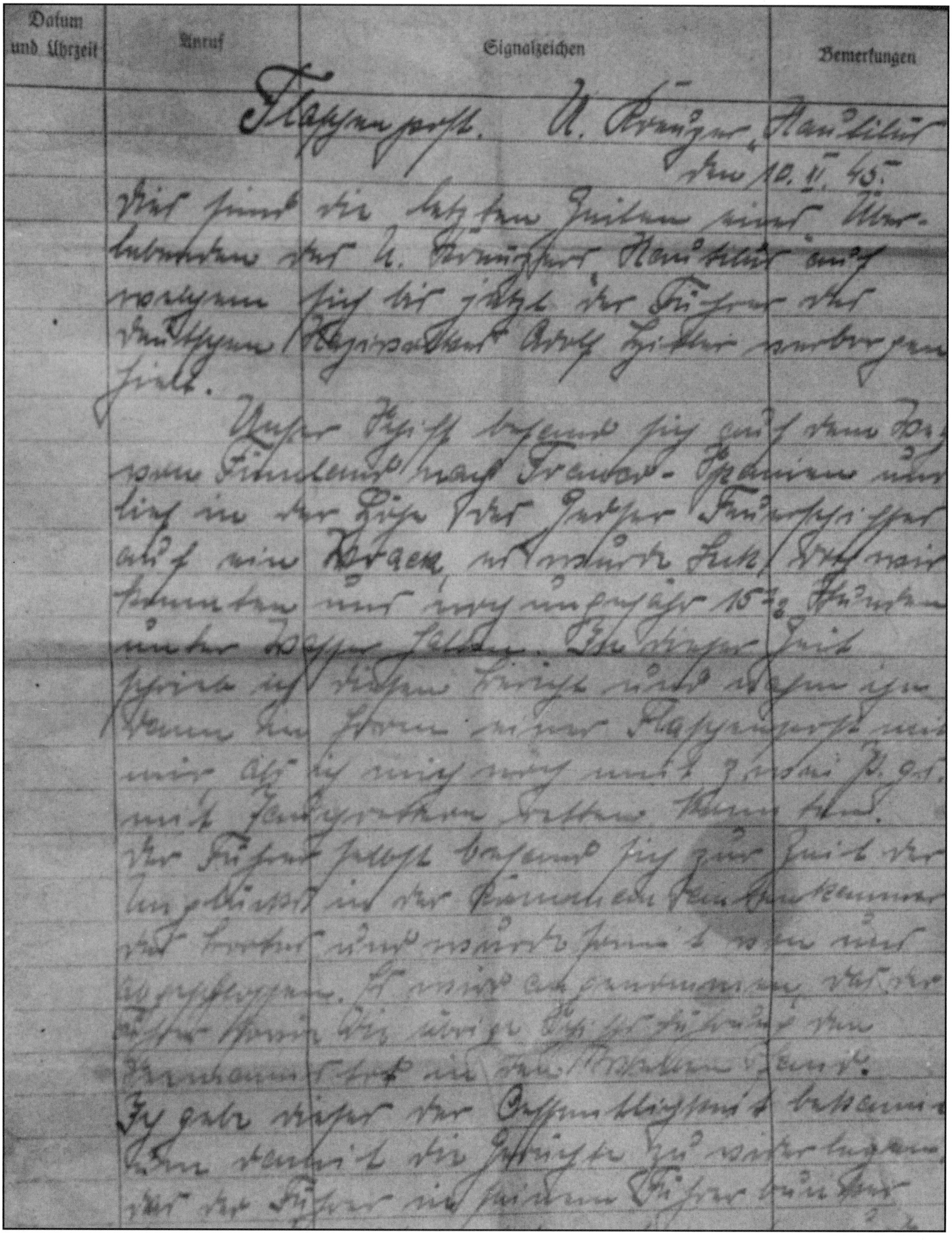

Datum und Uhrzeit	Anruf	Signalzeichen	Bemerkungen

Flaschenpost. U. Kreuzer Nautilus
den 10. II. 45.
Dies sind die letzten Zeilen eines Über-
lebenden des U. Kreuzer Nautilus [illegible]

[illegible]

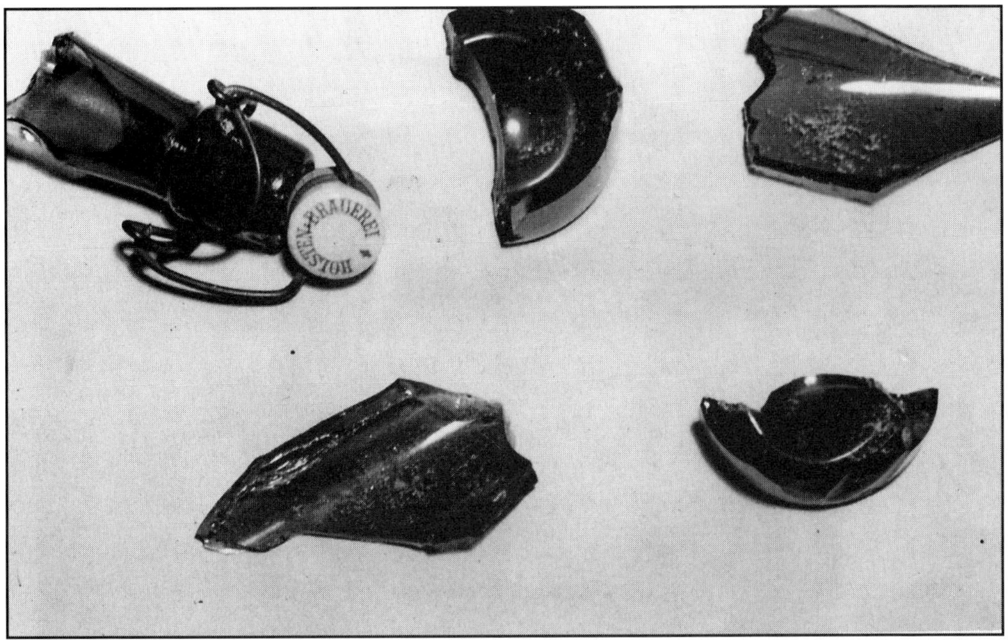

ABOVE: Hitler's bunker being demolished. East German troops blew up the bunker where Hitler planned the war, then committed suicide.

LEFT: A bottle containing a message claiming that Adolf Hitler drowned with a German U-boat.

FAR LEFT: The message in a bottle. Found in 1946, the note claims that Hitler did not die in Berlin, but sank with the U-boat Nauecilus.

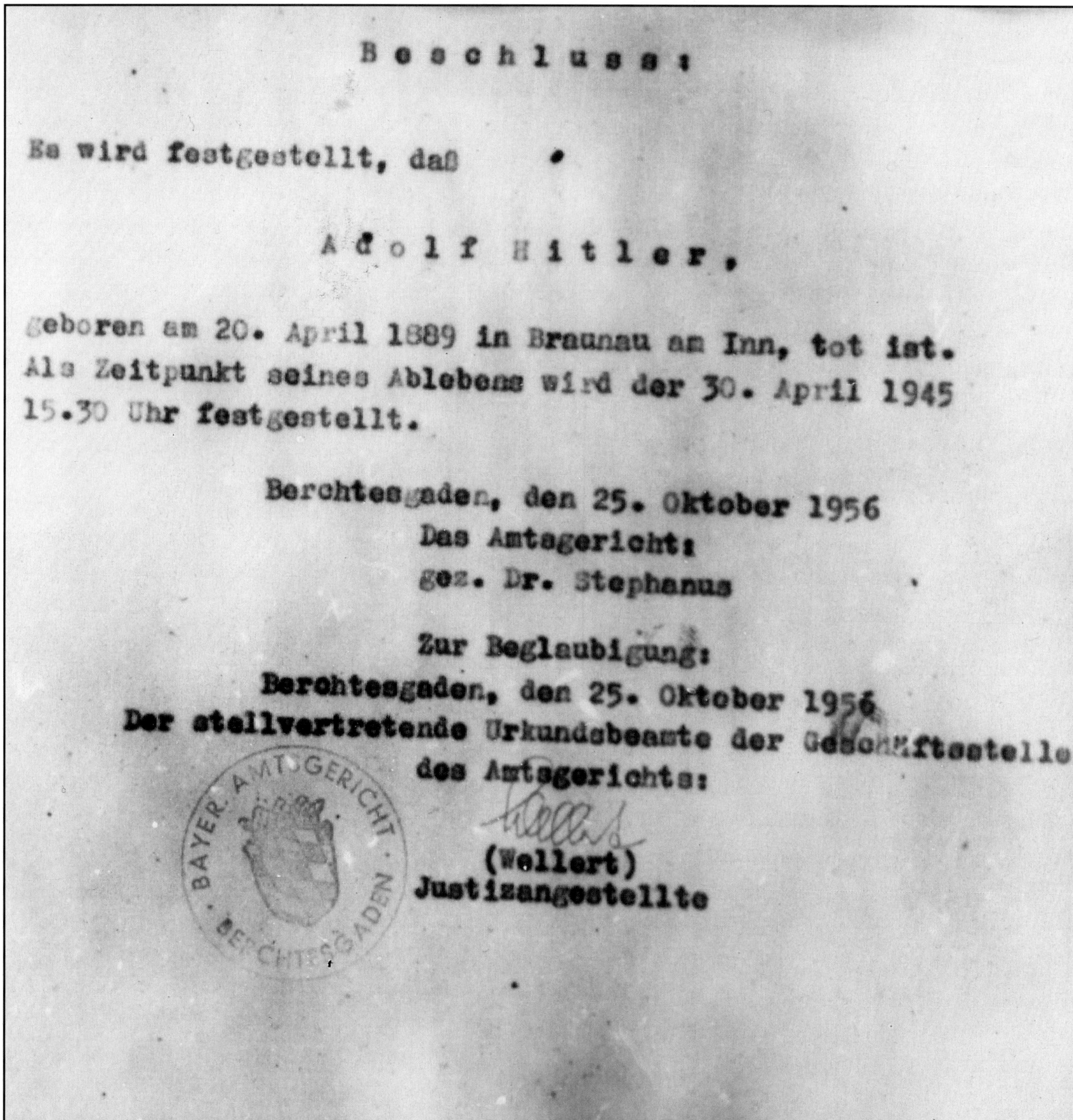

Beschluss:

Es wird festgestellt, daß

Adolf Hitler,

geboren am 20. April 1889 in Braunau am Inn, tot ist. Als Zeitpunkt seines Ablebens wird der 30. April 1945 15.30 Uhr festgestellt.

Berchtesgaden, den 25. Oktober 1956
Das Amtsgericht:
gez. Dr. Stephanus

Zur Beglaubigung:
Berchtesgaden, den 25. Oktober 1956
Der stellvertretende Urkundsbeamte der Geschäftsstelle des Amtsgerichts:

BAYER. AMTSGERICHT BERCHTESGADEN

(Wellert)
Justizangestellte

ABOVE: The official notice declaring Adolf Hitler dead. This was released from Berchtesgaden in 1956.

RIGHT: The official notice of Hitler's death posted in 1956.

PRINCIPAL DATES

1889 Born 20 April.

1903 Death of father, Alois.

1905 Move to Vienna.

1907 Death of mother, Klara.

1913 Move to Munich.

1914 Arrest for draft-dodging. Later declared unfit for military service. 1 August:World War I starts. 4 August: Joined Bavarian regiment. October: Action at Ypres. December: Awarded Iron Cross (Second Class).

1918 Awarded Iron Cross (First Class). November: Defeat of Germany.

1919 Joined German Workers' Party.

1923 Beer Hall Putsch. Wrote *Mein Kampf* in jail.

1927 First Nuremberg rally.

1928 Nazis won 12 seats in Reichstag.

1929 Wall Street Crash.

1930 Won 107 Reichstag seats, with 6.4 million votes.

1931 Stood against Hindenburg as President and secured 30.1 per cent of vote.

1933 Made Reich Chancellor. Reichstag Fire. Germany quit League of Nations.

1934 Night of the Long Knives. Death of Hindenburg. Hitler declared Führer.

1936 German Condor Legion fought in Spanish Civil War.

1937 First Autobahn built.

1938 German troops occupied demilitarised Rhineland. Anschluss of Austria. Sudetenland transferred to Germany.

1939 Czechoslovakian crisis. Munich conference. Occupation of Czechoslovakia. Invasion of Poland. Start of World War II.

1940 Invasion of Norway, Holland, Belgium, France. Battle of Britain.

1941 Operation Barbarossa – invasion of Russia. Final Solution (genocide of the Jews) agreed. War with America after Japanese attack on Pearl Harbour.

1942 Defeat in North Africa.

1943 Defeat at Stalingrad, Moscow, Kursk. Retreat from Russia.

1944 July Plot: Hitler survived bomb in his HQ. War in Italy.

1945 War in Germany. Suicide of Hitler and Eva Braun. German surrender.